Women's Inferior
Education

Blanche Fitzpatrick

The Praeger Special Studies program—utilizing the most modern and efficient book production techniques and a selective worldwide distribution network—makes available to the academic, government, and business communities significant, timely research in U.S. and international economic, social, and political development.

Women's Inferior Education

An Economic Analysis

Praeger Publishers New York Washington London

PRAEGER SPECIAL STUDIES IN U.S. ECONOMIC, SOCIAL, AND POLITICAL ISSUES

Library of Congress Cataloging in Publication Data

Fitzpatrick, Blanche E
  Women's inferior education.

  (Praeger special studies in U.S. economic, social,
and political issues)
  Bibliography: p.
  1. Education of women—Economic aspects—United States.
2. Discrimination in education—Economic aspects—United
States. 3. Education, Higher—United States. 4. Sex
discrimination against women—United States. I. Title.
LC1756.F5   376'.65'0973   76-2903
ISBN 0-275-56670-6

PRAEGER PUBLISHERS
111 Fourth Avenue, New York, N.Y. 10003, U.S.A.

Published in the United States of America in 1976
by Praeger Publishers, Inc.

Printed in the United States of America

This book is dedicated to

Ruth,
Judy, Kathy, Joyce, Joe, Jerry, Moire,
    Frank, John, Warren, Stephen,
Jessica, and Alyssa

in the hope that each succeeding generation
will find increasing educational opportunity.

PREFACE

As a faculty member at several colleges and universities since the 1950s, I realize that most teen-agers have little understanding of the routes within the education system leading to both white- and blue-collar jobs. There is growing awareness, however, that most women will now be in the labor market, working or seeking work, for 20 or 30 years, and that the amount of education and the type of education greatly affects both job and pay.

I served as chairwoman of the Task Force on Education of the Massachusetts Governor's Commission on the Status of Women, which made a study in 1972 of educational opportunities for girls and young women in Massachusetts. We found that at every level of academic and vocational education beyond high school young women did not have equal opportunity. Numbers of boys and girls graduating from high school were approximately equal. Yet there were four times as many places for men as for women in the new vocational-technical schools. Men predominated in enrollment at the universities, both public and private; while in the state colleges, with less chance for advanced and professional study, many more young women were enrolled.

Massachusetts is not unique in these respects. In order to provide young women and their parents with information on discriminatory admission policies, and discriminatory use of tax funds, I undertook research on enrollments in academic and vocational education in 20 states in 1973. With this information available, young women and their parents can take political action at local, state, and federal levels to insist on equal educational opportunity for the equally qualified.

Decisions made at age 17 need not set the pattern for life; there are many opportunities for reassessment along the way. It is highly desirable to provide opportunity for part-time and extension-type higher education for mature women with family responsibilities. When we see newspaper accounts of the 35-year-old mother of three who is entering law school, or of the 57-year-old grandmother who is receiving a bachelor's degree in the same class with her 21-year-old grandson, we can only applaud their courage and determination. But if more opportunities were provided for young women before they face the problems of combining child care, household operation, study, and a part-time job for needed income, both women and the U.S. economy would be better served. The average woman worker (full time) receives less than 60 percent of the pay of the average full-time male worker. The 20-year-old woman who is today being denied equal educational opportunity will be at age 50 an unskilled worker, most likely to be denied employment opportunities. We are faced with increasing problems of mental health among women left without a satisfying occupation after the children have grown.

In the lifelong struggle for economic survival, there are sufficient natural hurdles. In the case of women, additional barriers have been set up by leaders of American education--universities, colleges, vocational schools--that restrict most young women to training for lesser-paid skills, and to education for lower-paid professions. Young women often accept their lesser opportunities with youthful humility, and, reflecting a lifetime of societal put-downs, blame themselves for not achieving admission to the training and education desired. However, as they come to realize that they are victims of discrimination that affects not just the years of college or vocational training but lifelong opportunities for employment, they will resist being shunted to the lower track. Their parents also may take political action to assure that their tax money is being fairly distributed. The education of talented youth benefits not just the individual, but all of society. Especially if public funds are asked for support of education beyond high school, public and private institutions must guarantee all our youth equal opportunity for that education for which they are equally qualified.

ACKNOWLEDGMENTS

I would like to acknowledge the assistance and suggestions of the following individuals and agencies: Professors Everett J. Burtt, Jr. and John J. Hughes of the Boston University Department of Economics; Wendell D. Macdonald, regional commissioner, Edward T. O'Donnell, regional employment analyst, and Shirley Radlo, chief, Information and Correspondence Unit, of the U.S. Bureau of Labor Statistics, Boston; Elinor Rowe, associate commissioner, Massachusetts Department of Employment Security, Boston; Helen Yin, economist, U.S. Department of Commerce, Washington, D.C.; Lynn Kay and Leo Eiden of the U.S. Department of Health, Education, and Welfare, Office of Education, Washington, D.C.; Ellen Isenstein and Margaret Trocchio, reference librarians, Boston Public Library; Marie Lannon, senior reference librarian, Margaret Morris, head of technical services, and Malcolm Hamilton, vocational specialist, of the Gutman Library, Harvard University, Cambridge, Mass.; Scarvia B. Anderson of the Educational Testing Service, Princeton, N.J.; Theresa Phan-Thi-Ngoc-Chan of the Harvard Square Copying Service, Cambridge, Mass.; and the Program Support Branch, Division of Student Financial Aid, U.S. Office of Education, Washington, D.C.

CONTENTS

LIST OF TABLES AND FIGURES

Women's Inferior Education

1

WOMEN: A MINORITY
IN TAX-SUPPORTED
POSTSECONDARY EDUCATION

"I am being held back because I am a girl," her letter con-
cluded. The Massachusetts 14-year old, who had been denied admission to a publicly financed regional vocational school, addressed
the letter "To Whom it May Concern" and sent it to the State House
in Boston.[1] It can be said fairly that her letter concerns girls and
young women from snowbound Maine to sunny California who are
similarly denied opportunity for vocational and higher education beyond high school and thus are being programmed for a lifetime of
dead-end jobs. Her letter concerns parents, some of whom may accept the myth that a good education is less important for a daughter
than for a son. Her letter concerns the leaders of American education who have not led in ending sex discrimination in education.

It is asking too much of a teen-age girl to expect that she can,
by herself, discover the institutionalized sex discrimination that lies
ahead. The high school junior or senior, whether in Wichita or
Rockford, in San Bernadino or Yonkers, in Scranton or El Paso,
does not have a clear picture of the structure of the U.S. educational
system beyond high school. The routes to the skilled trades and professions are hard to find. By contrast, the routes to unskilled and
semiskilled jobs lie invitingly close at hand. A quick shift from high
school to a full-time paying job may overcome any disappointment at
being denied education beyond high school. Yet the 17-year-old girl
all too quickly becomes the 35-year-old woman channeled by educational discrimination into low-paid dead-end jobs for the rest of her
working life--that is, for 20 or 30 years.

This is not to say that the American education system should
or could produce all chiefs and no Indians. It is only to question why
that system produces so few women chiefs and pours out such quanti-
ties of women Indians--secretary, salesgirl, nurse, teacher, all
employed in fields where top administrators are men.

Equal opportunity for education beyond high school will not guarantee high lifetime income to young women. Neither will lack of education prevent those with unusual drive and ability from winning some measure of fame and fortune. Yet it is highly unlikely that one will become a successful doctor or lawyer without appropriate education; it is equally difficult to master a skilled craft without an expert teacher. Thus for most 17-year olds, specialized education beyond high school is the necessary route to skills that improve lifetime job satisfaction and income. Under the illusion that educational opportunities were equally available to all young people, women in later years often blame themselves for "missing out" on earlier chances. Yet it is an illusion that both sexes have equal educational opportunity. This myth is fostered by the competitive grade-oriented atmosphere of public high schools that leads the student to believe that a great sorting process will distribute high school graduates according to ability--to top universities, to four-year liberal arts colleges, to two-year community colleges, to vocational training, or to no further education. Family income may be recognized as a limiting factor, but a vague notion of available scholarships may encourage the poor bright girl as well as the poor bright boy to dream of admission to a top university--usually, to dream in vain.

A recent Department of Labor study of the education and employment status of young women 14 to 24 bore the title Years for Decision,[2] implying that the choice for further education rests with young women. Actually, the nation's leaders have in fact already made the decision to provide fewer places for young women than for young men in education beyond high school, and within each education sector to restrict most women to second-ranked schools and lesser skills, leading to lower-paid occupations.

This administrative decision has been made by college and university trustees, college presidents, directors of vocational schools, state commissioners of education, and men of similar stature. The decision is not questioned by parents or other adults who are understandably preoccupied by rising prices, taxes, unemployment, or government scandals and who have little time to examine the admission policies of local or distant vocational schools, colleges, and universities.

Yet these admissions policies ensure that most women will be channeled toward overcrowded, low-paid, dead-end jobs during their working lives. The average woman working full time, year round, in 1974 earned only 57 percent of the income of the male worker similarly employed ($6,490 vs. $11,383). Women are in fact losing ground, since the same comparison in 1959 showed women's income as 64 percent of the comparable male income.[3]

Even loving parents may in some instances question the need of further education for a girl who "is sure to be married in a year or two." The majority of parents of today's high school seniors are between 40 and 60 years of age. Very likely they themselves were children of nonworking mothers. In 1930 women (most of them young and single) were only about one-fifth of the U.S. labor force. With high unemployment levels during the 1930s depression, married women were often denied opportunity for employment, even in the public school systems.

In the 1970s however, women (the majority older and married) are over two-fifths of the labor force.[4] With smaller families the rule, the average woman worker today may expect to spend 20 or 30 years in the labor force. Over such a time span education is essential to prepare for better-paid, as well as more interesting, lifetime careers.

Most young women will marry within ten years of their graduation from high school. In the past 15 years, young persons for a variety of reasons are remaining single longer. About one-half of young women 21 years of age were single in 1974, as compared to about one-third in 1964. Since about one-half of current graduating seniors go on to college, and 82 percent of young women aged 18 were single in the 1974 study, marital status is becoming less of a factor in plans for further education.[5] Moreover, as pointed out in the Occupational Outlook Quarterly for Summer 1973, one woman in ten will be widowed before age 50; three marriages in ten now end in divorce.[6] About two-thirds of working women in 1974 were supporting themselves or contributing to the support of children or other dependents. Of this group, 19 percent of working women were widowed, divorced, or separated; 23 percent were single; in addition, an estimated 22 percent had husbands whose incomes were below $9,000 at a time when a low standard of living for a family of four was estimated at $9,198.[7] (See Figure 1.1.)

Many parents have simply not recognized the changing lifetime employment patterns for women and also seem to be unaware that their taxes are financing the education of the boy next door, while their daughter loses out because so few places are provided for girls. Not every boy or girl is academically qualified for university or college, or has the aptitude for training in the skilled trades. The overburdened taxpayer may not be able to support universal education beyond high school. But if we ask, "Are the present educational opportunities beyond high school being distributed according to ability?" the answer is, flatly, "No."

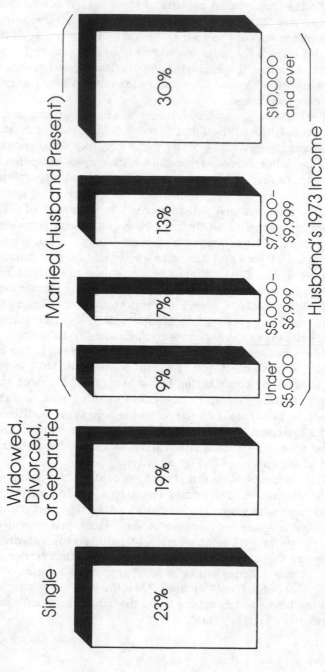

FIGURE 1.1

Economic Need of Women to Work

(women in the labor force, by marital status, March 1974)

Single

Widowed,
Divorced,
or Separated

Married (Husband Present)

23%

19%

9%   7%   13%   30%

Under $5,000- $7,000- $10,000
$5,000 $6,999 $9,999   and over

Husband's 1973 Income

Source: Prepared by the Women's Bureau, Employment Standards Administration, from data published by the Bureau of Labor Statistics, U. S. Department of Labor.

WOMEN'S QUALIFICATIONS FOR
POSTSECONDARY EDUCATION

Is this because girls are less qualified? There is no evidence for this belief, so widely held by women as well as men. On the contrary, in academic courses girls consistently receive higher grades than boys. "Studies going back as far as 1929 show better grades for females from elementary school through college," as Patricia Cross notes, quoting references from Anastasi and Foley's Differential Psychology. A study of 400 children in grades 2-6 by Lentz in 1929 found girls consistently excelled in school grades when compared with boys receiving the same achievement test scores. A 1947 study of a single high school, by Lobaugh, for each of the four years found "the percentage of As and Bs larger, and the percentage of Ds and Fs smaller among the girls than among the boys."[8] More recent studies bear out the findings. At the college level, Bayer, Royer, and Webb, in a 1971 study of (1967) freshmen, found 14 percent of women reporting graduation with honors, compared to 11 percent of young men (different courses taken not noted).[9] In the Aptitude Testing Program (ATP) Questionnaire administered by the College Entrance Examination Board, in connection with the 1974 SAT (Scholastic Achievement Test) examination, girls reported slightly more As and Bs than did boys. Even in high school mathematics, in contradiction to the stereotype, girls achieve better grades than boys; this reflects a smaller number of very bright girls taking advanced high school math, in comparison with a large number of boys, spread over the I.Q. spectrum.[10] (The latest data on course distribution indicate that more girls are now taking four or more years of high school mathematics--59 percent of boys and 37 percent of girls, as reported on the ATP questionnaire.)[11]

Girls historically have scored better than boys on the verbal aptitude portions of the college entrance tests, with boys higher on the mathematical portion. In the past decade however, scores for both sexes have declined; with a larger number of girls now taking the test, girls in the 1974 examination scored slightly below boys on the verbal and considerably below on the mathematical portion (reflecting the different percentages of each sex taking advanced mathematics, as noted above).

Similar findings were made in four areas by the National Assessment of Educational Progress, comparing the test performances of the sexes at ages 9, 13, 17, and 26-35. Females had the advantage in reading and writing, males in citizenship and science.[12] These differences in test scores reflect the different courses of study pursued by boys and girls in the public education system, encouraged by sex-differentiated programs of study.

TABLE 1.1

Opportunities for Women in Education Beyond High School
in the United States

	Men	Women	Total	Women as Percent
1973 high school graduates[1]	1,353,000	1,377,000	2,730,000	50
I. Academic (degree credit) enrollment				
Fall 1973 full-time undergraduate enrollment, public and private (nonprofit), U.S. total	2,817,598	2,213,261	5,030,859	44
A. Research universities,* total[2]	619,433	424,811	1,044,244	41
Public	521,154	366,891	888,045	41
Private	98,279	57,920	156,199	37
B. Excluding research universities				
Public, total	2,080,432	1,615,286	3,695,718	44
Universities	343,711	289,362	633,073	46
Other four-year	728,220	636,670	1,364,890	47
Two-year	487,347	322,363	809,710	40
Private, total	737,166	597,975	1,335,141	45
Universities	107,533	76,659	184,192	42
Other four-year	495,997	424,996	920,993	46
Two-year	35,357	38,400	73,757	52
II. Vocational enrollment				
A. Fiscal year 1974 enrollment in state-approved postsecondary vocational, total (unduplicated)[3]	n.a.	n.a.	1,552,779	40+[4]
Occupations:				
Trade and industry			412,669	13
Technical			231,387	8
Home economics (gainful)			46,308	84
Health			228,180	92
Office			426,346	62
Distributive			133,214	26
Other			74,675	n.a.
B. Fall 1973 full- and part-time nondegree-credit enrollment, public and private (nonprofit)[5]	603,774	488,370	1,092,144	45
in public two-year	543,006	431,429	974,435	44
C. Calendar year 1974 registered apprenticeships[6]	288,487	2,562	291,049	.9
Calendar year 1972 joint labor-management apprenticeships reported to EEOC[7]	93,802	308	94,110	.3
D. Fiscal year MDTA training[8]				
Institutional	73,300	37,100	110,400	34
JOBS Optional/On-the-job Training	49,344	13,756	63,100	22[4]

6

Notes to Table 1.1

n.a. = not available.

*Research universities are defined by the Carnegie Commission on Higher Education as those institutions among the 100 leading institutions in federal financial support over a period of years who awarded at least 50 Ph.D.s (or M.D.s) in 1969-70. See the commission's A Classification of Institutions of Higher Education (Berkeley, Calif.: Carnegie Commission, 1973), pp. 2-3.

†National postsecondary breakdown by sex, fiscal year 1969.

‡National JOBS Optional/On-the-Job Training by sex, fiscal year 1974.

Note: Percentages computed by the author.

Sources:

1. U.S. Department of Health, Education, and Welfare, Statistics of Elementary and Secondary Day Schools, Fall 1973 (Washington, D.C., March 1971), Table 8, p. 25.

2. U.S. Department of Health, Education, and Welfare, Fall Enrollment in Higher Education, 1973 (Washington, D.C., 1975), Tables 2, 3, 4, 10 (A-N), 13 (A-N), 20.

3. U.S. Department of Health, Education, and Welfare, Vocational and Technical Education, Fiscal Year 1974 (Washington, D.C., 1974); and idem, Vocational Education Information III (Washington, D.C., 1974), Tables 042-050.

4. U.S. Department of Health, Education, and Welfare, Vocational and Technical Education, Fiscal Year 1969 (Washington, D.C., 1969). (This is the latest annual report with breakdown by sex and program.)

5. U.S. Department of Health, Education, and Welfare, Fall Enrollment in Higher Education, 1973 (Washington, D.C., 1975), Table 10, p. 59.

6. Computer printout distributed by U.S. Department of Labor, Bureau of Apprenticeship and Training, March 1976.

7. Unpublished data from Technical Information Division, Office of Research, Equal Employment Opportunity Commission, Washington, D.C., 1973.

8. U.S. Department of Labor, Manpower Report of the President, 1975 (Washington, D.C., 1975), Tables F-2, F-4, F-9.

In technical and trade occupations, when a girl or woman does break through the barriers of discriminatory admissions, she performs as well as her male counterparts. A few women have followed the trail blazed by Rosie the Riveter in World War II; the Department of Labor reported in 1970 nearly 2,000 women holding apprenticeships in fields ranging from carpentry to jet engine assembly. [13] But although women may be equally qualified for academic and vocational education beyond high school, they are not given equal opportunity to develop their skills. Let us look at the distribution of postsecondary students and trainees in the 1973-74 academic year. (Enrollments at institutions of higher education are reported as of fall 1973; vocational enrollments cover fiscal year 1974, which runs from July 1, 1973 to June 30, 1974; apprenticeships are reported for calendar years 1972 and 1974.)

PERCENTAGE OF WOMEN IN TAX-SUPPORTED ACADEMIC AND VOCATIONAL SCHOOLS BEYOND HIGH SCHOOL

Bearing in mind that women are just about half the high school graduates nationally, we can see in Tables 1.1 and 1.2 that a much smaller percent go on to further education leading to careers in skilled trades and professions.

In academic (degree-credit) programs beyond high school (Table 1.1, section I), women were 44 percent of full-time undergraduate enrollment in fall 1973. They were, however, only 41 percent of enrollment in public "research universities" and 37 percent in private "research universities," the major route to professional careers. The percentage of women was highest in enrollment at public "other four-year" institutions (47 percent) that in the past have tended to concentrate on teacher-training; and in two-year private institutions (52 percent), often more socially oriented, which enroll less than 2 percent of all full-time undergraduates.

In vocational programs beyond high school (Table 1.1, section II) women as a percentage of enrollment ranged from less than 1 percent of registered apprentices to 45 percent of nonbachelor's degree programs of higher education, as discussed below.

Part A of section I reports total full- and part-time enrollment for fiscal year 1974 in state-approved postsecondary programs in public and private two- and four-year higher education, area vocational-technical postsecondary schools, combined secondary/postsecondary schools, and technical institutes, as reported annually by each state to the U.S. Department of Education. These annual reports provide no breakdown later than 1969 of enrollment by sex

within programs. The 1969 distribution of such state-approved programs indicated that women were only 40 percent of enrollment, and
as will be discussed in Chapter 2, women were found most concentrated in office and health-technician programs, rather than in training for higher paid jobs through the trades and industry program.

More recent studies of major subareas of postsecondary vocational education indicate that this pattern persists. Preliminary results of a 1974 Office of Civil Rights study of public postsecondary
area vocational schools, with over 0.5 million enrollment in January
1974, reported that men constituted 60 percent of the total enrollment, with two-thirds of the men in trades and technical fields, and
more than two-thirds of the women students in business programs
and health fields.[14] These tax-supported schools, mainly built over
the past 10 to 15 years, have in fact often been built with the intent
of serving an all-male student body; those schools that admit women
often restrict enrollment to a small number of programs.

Likewise, preliminary reports of a 1973-74 study by the National Center for Educational Statistics (NCES) of noncollegiate postsecondary schools, with occupational programs enrolling 1.3 million
students (exclusive of correspondence schools) showed men as 59
percent of enrollment in public institutions, though only 46 percent in
private schools. In the tax-supported public institutions men were
93 percent of enrollment in technical programs, and 87 percent of
enrollment in trades and industrial programs; women were 91 percent of enrollment in health programs, and 83 percent of enrollment
in business/office programs[15] (see Table 2.4, p. 50).

Part B of Table 1.1 shows women as 45 percent of enrollment
in fall 1973 in nonbachelor's-degree-credit programs at two- and
four-year institutions, public and private nonprofit. Distribution of
men and women among programs appears similar to that noted above.*

---

*There is duplication that cannot be clearly identified by re-
porting agencies between enrollments under A and B, section II, of
Table 1.1. The total postsecondary enrollment of 1,552,779 for fiscal year 1974 includes only those vocational programs funded and/or
approved by the appropriate state agencies; on the other hand, officials of the U.S. Office of Education indicate that not all of the
1,092,144 nondegree-credit enrollment reported by institutions of
higher education may actually consist only of formal vocational programs. The U.S. Office of Education questionnaire defines "nonbachelor's-degree-credit" programs as "organized occupational
curriculums of less than four years, primarily in the vocational and
technical fields, not chiefly creditable toward a bachelor's degree.
[These programs are] normally terminal and result in formal

Women were just under 1 percent (.9 percent) of registered apprentices under federal programs in 1974 (Table 1.1, section II, C). In the joint union-management-sponsored apprenticeship programs covering five or more apprentices, women were only .3 percent of the total reported to the Equal Employment Opportunity Commission in 1972. In apprenticeships women are concentrated in the cosmetologist program, rather than in the traditional skilled trades in construction and metalworking.

The federally sponsored "Manpower" programs (recently renamed Employment and Training Programs) are likewise predominantly male (Table 1.1, section II, D). The fiscal year 1974 Manpower Development and Training Act (MDTA) institutional training program was 66 percent men; the JOP/OJT (JOBS Optional/On-the-job Training) program was 78 percent men. (Other federal training programs under the Employment and Training Act have not been shown in Table 1.1 because they combine unknown amounts of training in conjunction with counseling, remedial studies, and income supplements--that is, Neighborhood Youth Corps, Operation Mainstream, etc.) Men predominated in the programs classified as "skill training"; according to a recent analysis of the impact of manpower programs by faculty of the Wharton School, "minority and female trainees were heavily concentrated in programs having a limited emphasis on the acquisition and development of marketable occupational skills."[16] For example, women (frequently "welfare mothers") were 72 percent of enrollment in the Work Incentive Program (WIN); "a tax credit was made available to private employers [in 1971] to facilitate placement of WIN participants." The 1974 Manpower Report reviewing program development comments: "An unanswered query is whether the tax credit is largely benefiting employers rather than opening up jobs with opportunities for training and advancement for welfare recipients. Limited information suggests that a majority of the 25,000 participants hired were placed in service and clerical jobs with wages of $1.60 to

---

recognition such as a certificate or diploma." The latest reported "formal awards based on organized curriculums at the technical or semi-professional level" (see Table B.3) showed women as 60 percent of the 1972 recipients in less-than-two-year programs, and only 42 percent of recipients in programs requiring two or more years. Women received 92 percent of awards in health fields, 54 percent of awards in business programs, and only 1 percent of awards in mechanical and engineering technologies (U.S. Department of Health, Education, and Welfare, Fall Enrollment in Higher Education, 1973 [Washington, D.C., 1975], p. 1053).

$2.00 an hour, the sort of jobs normally available to unskilled people."[17]

The demonstrated inequality between the sexes in education and training beyond high school, drawn from the approximately equal numbers of boy and girl high school graduates, is reason enough to examine American education patterns more closely. Just as war is too important a matter to be left to the generals, education is too important to be left to the professional educators. From Table 1.1 we can see that over 1 million young women in 1973 did not have access to the educational opportunities for which they were as well qualified as their brothers.

WOMEN'S RESTRICTED OPPORTUNITIES

But the difference in numbers greatly understates the discrimination in development of youthful talent. Because of the unequal distribution of the sexes among types of institutions, young women are being channeled toward lower-ranked and lower-paid occupations, as shown in Tables 1.2, 1.3, and 1.4, and in Figure 1.2. The young women at the two-year community college or four-year teacher's college do not have an equal chance with the young men undergraduates at the prestigious universities with respect to careers in law, medicine, scholarly research, and government. The few women admitted to the modern vocational-technical schools are encouraged to take programs in medical technology or cosmetology, but are directed away from metalworking or carpentry.

As we will discuss further in Chapter 2, it is the difference in the courses available to young women, as well as in the institutions attended by them, that makes for lifetime inequality of status and income. While young men are directed toward "career ladders," young women may more accurately be pictured as ascending "step stools," where the top level leaves them stranded for a low-paid lifetime.

In the otherwise excellent article, "Career Planning for High School Girls" in Occupational Outlook Quarterly cited above, young women are advised to broaden their horizons, to recognize that public schoolteachers will be in oversupply through the 1970s, and to choose instead one of the expected "shortage" occupations. Yet the article nowhere points out the lamentable and obvious discrimination that effectively bars young women from the access roads to these careers. For example:

While the article points out that Chemists with Ph.D.s "will be in strong demand during the decade,"

- it is nowhere pointed out that fewer women are admitted to universities, and thus fewer will aspire or be admitted to graduate study (see Table 1.1).

While the comment is made regarding Physicians that "prospects in this shortage occupation are likely to be excellent through the 1970s,"

- it is not pointed out that the smaller numbers of women admitted to top universities limits the number who will aspire and be admitted to professional schools (see Tables 1.1 and 1.2).

While the article suggests that for Carpentry, "Most training authorities say that the best way to prepare for the building trades is through apprenticeship programs,"

- it is not pointed out that women are reported to be less than 1 percent of apprentices. (See tables for individual states, Chapter 3, and Table B.1.)

With respect to Welding, the article suggests that "Persons interested in this field should take high school or vocational school classes in welding methods,"

- although girls and young women are often denied admission to public vocational schools, or have access to only a limited group of courses (cosmetology, typing) in others (see Table 1.1, section II, A).

Regarding Appliance Service, it is suggested that "workers may receive training through high school vocational courses or through federal job training programs for unemployed or underemployed workers,"

- yet in fact, enrollment of girls in high school vocational courses is concentrated in home economics and office occupations (59 percent and 34 percent respectively of all 1969 secondary vocational female enrollment).[18]

- In postsecondary vocational programs, 48 percent of total female enrollment was in office occupations; 30 percent in health fields; and only 8 percent in trades and industry in 1969. (Table 2.2 below.)

● In federal training programs, consistently over the past ten years, women have averaged only about 40 percent of those admitted to MDTA institutional training, and here also were channeled to health aide or clerical training programs, rather than to the skilled, higher-paid trades.[19]

This restriction of educational opportunity, and thus of career opportunity, leads directly to the economic disadvantage of women through working life, as indicated in Tables 1.3 and 1.4. As a result of discrimination in the education system, only small percentages of women are found throughout the top 20 percent of occupations ranked by male median earnings in 1969, and high percentages of women in the bottom 20 percent of the same ranking.

TABLE 1.2

Women as a Percentage of Degree-Credit Undergraduate, Graduate, and First-Professional Enrollment

	Men	Women	Total	Women as Percent
1973 U.S. degree-credit enrollment by level (full time)				
Undergraduate	2,817,598	2,213,261	5,030,859	44
Graduate	273,123	137,623	410,746	34
First professional	173,137	30,514	203,651	15
1972 U.S. degree recipients				
Law (LL.B, J.D.)	20,472	1,545	22,017	7
Medicine (M.D.)	8,486	845	9,331	9
Education (total)				
Bachelor's	49,876	142,492	192,368	74
Master's	41,925	56,355	98,280	57
Doctorate	5,381	1,660	7,041	24

Sources: U.S. Department of Health, Education, and Welfare, National Center for Educational Statistics, Fall Enrollment in Higher Education, 1973 (Washington, D.C., 1975); and idem, Earned Degrees Conferred, 1971-72 (Washington, D.C., 1972), Table 8, pp. 180-81, Table 9, pp. 733-35.

TABLE 1.3

Selected Occupations of Men and Women, Ranked by 1969 Median Earnings, Top 20 Percent

Men

Rank	Occupation	Median annual earnings	Median age	Median school years completed	Percent completing at least 4 years of high school	Percent completing at least 4 years of college	Percent employed[f] the full year	Percent of women in the occupation
Top decile								
1	Physicians, medical and osteopathic	25,000+	44.3	17+	99.7	97.3	74.5	9.0
2	Dentists	21,687	45.5	17+	99.4	96.0	56.2	3.0
3	Judges	21,529	56.8	17+	92.8	75.5	75.5	5.1
4	Lawyers	18,749	42.8	17+	99.3	94.1	83.1	4.8
5	College and university teachers, law	18,161	40.6	17+	99.5	97.9	61.5	6.6
6	College and university teachers, health specialties	17,884	47.6	17+	97.3	96.2	73.7	47.4
7	Optometrists	17,398	47.5	17+	97.3	85.5	80.8	4.1
8	Airplane pilots	17,306	40.8	14.2	94.1	27.7	82.8	1.0
9	Veterinarians	16,505	35.0	17+	98.3	95.4	86.2	5.7
10	Actuaries	15,629	35.9	16.7	99.5	87.3	81.9	28.3
11	Physicists and astronomers	15,242	40.2	16.7	99.3	90.3	87.6	4.3
12	Aeronautical and astronautical engineers	14,888		16.4	97.4	63.9	90.0	1.5
	Managers and administrators, nec.—salaried:							
13	Durable goods manufacturing	14,829	44.6	14.1	86.0	35.9	92.5	3.5
14	Podiatrists	14,787	49.2	17+	98.6	84.1	70.0	9.5
15	Sales managers, except retail trade	14,526	42.9	14.5	90.9	37.0	92.2	3.5
16	Dental hygienists	14,291	47.2	12.7	69.3	14.4	85.1	93.2
17	College and university teachers, education	14,248	42.2	17+	99.6	96.9	57.5	29.3
18	Mathematicians	14,241	33.0	17+	99.9	89.7	82.9	24.5
19	College and university teachers, psychology	14,220	37.0	17+	99.7	97.4	60.5	29.7
	Managers and administrators, nec.—self-employed:							
20	Finance, insurance, real estate	14,155	52.0	14.5	84.8	37.7	82.3	10.6
	Managers and administrators, nec.—salaried:							
21	Nondurable goods manufacturing	14,028	45.4	13.9	84.0	36.6	91.8	6.2
22	Chemical engineers	14,004	39.0	16.8	98.4	86.9	87.9	1.1
23	Life and physical scientists, nec.	13,997	37.7	17+	98.3	86.2	87.0	20.9
24	School administrators, college	13,938	44.0	17+	95.3	79.8	82.6	23.0
25	Atmospheric and space scientists	13,901	44.4	16.3	97.0	57.9	92.5	10.1
26	College and university teachers, engineering	13,898	38.4	17+	99.2	92.0	67.6	6.0
27	Economists	13,780	37.9	16.7	97.8	75.1	84.9	11.5
28	Geologists	13,641	41.1	17+	99.2	90.3	68.4	3.6
29	Metallurgical and material engineers	13,619	39.9	16.5	97.7	69.2	88.3	.8
30	Political scientists	13,588	34.7	17+	97.1	79.5	79.8	26.1
31	Petroleum engineers	13,572	39.8	16.6	96.9	77.5	90.1	6.9
32	Stock and bond salesmen	13,565	39.5	16.2	77.5	55.9	82.7	8.7
33	Mechanical engineers	13,488	41.4	16.3	92.3	58.0	55.9	1.0
34	Electrical and electronic engineers	13,417	38.3	16.3	96.6	60.8	89.4	1.7
35	Sales engineers	13,328	41.4	16.1	95.7	52.5	90.3	.7
	Managers and administrators, nec.—salaried:							
36	Finance, insurance, real estate	13,322	43.3	15.1	90.3	43.0	90.3	14.6
37	School administrators, elementary and secondary	13,191	44.0	17+	98.7	93.8	64.3	26.9
38	Architects	13,188	40.7	17.0	95.1	74.4	82.6	3.7
39	Marine scientists	13,188	38.5	17.0	98.6	76.7	91.1	4.6
40	Air traffic controllers	13,021	37.3	12.7	91.3	6.7	92.4	4.8

14

No.	Occupation							
43	Psychologists	12,884	36.7	17+	98.9	95.7	69.9	35.9
44	Computer specialists, nec.	12,873	34.2	15.9	98.5	43.3	91.8	13.2
45	Managers and administrators, nec.—salaried: Construction.	12,795	45.1	12.5	66.1	11.1	84.8	1.8
46	Civil engineers.	12,790	40.9	16.3	93.7	63.4	88.4	1.5
47	Engineers, nec.	12,783	40.0	16.2	95.2	54.9	87.8	1.7
48	Managers and administrators, nec.—salaried: Communications, utilities, and sanitary services	12,741	45.1	13.0	85.0	26.7	93.0	10.7
49	College and university teachers, chemistry.	12,693	35.2	17+	99.9	97.0	64.1	11.6
50	College and university teachers, agriculture.	12,660	43.2	17+	99.1	95.0	79.9	4.9
51	Computer systems analysts.	12,600	33.3	16.1	97.5	5.6	90.0	13.9
52	Managers and administrators, nec.—salaried: Wholesale trade	12,464	45.8	12.9	81.2	23.8	91.4	4.6
53	Managers and administrators, nec.—salaried: Business and repair services.	12,393	41.6	13.5	82.7	32.5	88.7	11.5
54	College and university teachers, social science, nec.	12,248	37.6	17+	99.8	97.0	48.9	20.9
55	College and university teachers, biology.	12,192	37.0	17+	99.6	96.1	59.0	21.8
56	College and university teachers, business and commerce.	12,120	38.5	17+	99.8	95.4	54.3	31.8
57	Industrial engineers.	12,089	41.3	15.7	94.0	47.9	89.4	3.0
58	Health administrators.	12,087	46.1	16.1	89.7	51.6	89.8	44.8
59	Pharmacists.	12,065	43.1	16.6	97.1	75.5	84.5	12.0
60	Mining engineers.	12,025	41.2	16.4	91.4	64.5	84.6	1.1
61	Managers and administrators, nec.—self-employed: Communications, utilities, and sanitary services	11,971	48.7	12.2	55.1	11.8	77.6	7.7
62	College and university teachers, physics.	11,958	34.5	17+	99.1	85.5	60.3	4.3
63	Chiropractors.	11,957	46.7	16.8	97.5	83.9	79.8	8.0
64	Managers and administrators nec.—salaried: All other industries.	11,907	44.3	15.2	85.3	45.1	83.5	20.1
65	College and university teachers, atmospheric, earth, marine, and space sciences	11,834	34.6	17+	99.9	94.8	57.1	11.4
66	Bank officers and financial managers.	11,742	40.1	15.0	94.8	41.2	90.3	17.5
67	Public relations men and publicity writers.	11,713	42.0	15.9	93.9	49.2	83.9	26.6
68	Chemists.	11,570	38.9	16.7	95.9	72.7	78.3	11.9
69	Urban and regional planners.	11,544	38.5	17.0	97.7	75.1	82.1	10.5
70	Locomotive engineers.	11,530	51.8	12.0	51.5	1.2	81.4	.9
71	Operations and systems researchers and analysts.	11,453	38.6	14.6	93.1	38.0	90.5	9.1
72	Personnel and labor relations workers.	11,449	40.7	15.4	92.0	45.9	88.5	31.5
73	Managers and administrators, nec.—salaried: Nondurable goods manufacturing.	11,427	45.4	12.7	76.5	16.6	90.6	11.7
74	Officials of lodges, societies, and unions.	11,397	46.9	12.8	72.7	25.5	86.4	16.5
75	Officials and administrators, Federal public administration and postal service.	11,352	48.2	13.9	85.5	35.6	91.0	18.8
76	Designers.	11,155	37.5	14.1	89.4	30.4	83.0	24.1
77	Sales representatives, manufacturing.	11,124	41.0	13.6	85.9	29.0	85.8	8.8
78	College and university teachers, sociology.	11,097	36.7	17+	99.	98.3	55.6	26.6
79	Statisticians.	10,985	38.6	16.4	96.	62.6	84.4	40.3
80	Clerical supervisors, nec.	10,865	45.6	12.9	85.9	22.5	92.0	43.0
81	College and university teachers, history.	10,833	35.9	17+	99.2	98.3	48.9	17.9
82	Authors.	10,823	40.9	15.9	95.6	49.2	74.1	30.5
83	Railroad conductors.	10,801	51.5	12.1	56.5	1.2	80.5	1.0
84	Advertising agents and salesmen.	10,289	43.6	14.4	90.5	34.1	79.4	20.7

(continued)

(Table 1.3 continued)

Women

Rank	Occupation	Median annual earnings	Median age	Median school years completed	Percent completing at least 4 years of high school	Percent completing at least 4 years of college	Percent employed the full year	Percent of women in the occupation
	Top decile							
1	Sales engineers	13,181	45.3	16.0	95.2	49.7	86.0	0.7
2	Mechanical engineers	11,377	36.9	15.6	91.9	46.6	73.4	1.0
3	Locomotive engineers	11,063	51.4	12.1	57.2		90.8	.9
4	Aeronautical and astronautical engineers	10,448	39.6	15.0	83.2	42.7	74.3	1.5
5	Chemical engineers	10,023	24.5	16.6	96.2	81.5	77.7	1.1
6	Electrical and electronic engineers	9,813	40.4	15.2	91.8	46.5	82.4	1.7
7	Physicians, medical and osteopathic	9,788	40.4	17+	97.3	81.6	64.5	9.0
8	Millwrights	9,725	43.7	11.5	45.0	4.3	78.9	1.2
9	College and university teachers, physics	9,589	34.1	17+	99.9	87.8	41.6	4.3
10	Engineers, nec.	9,528	34.6	15.9	91.2	49.4	75.3	1.7
11	Civil engineers	9,363	36.4	16.1	95.5	53.9	75.7	1.5
12	Managers and administrators, nec.—salaried: Construction	9,344	47.5	12.5	69.6	9.5	83.2	1.8
13	Airplane pilots	9,240	38.8	13.9	95.8	13.8	73.0	1.0
14	Physicists and astronomers	9,071	36.4	17.0	99.9	83.6	74.3	4.3
15	College and university teachers, education	9,018	42.1	17+	99.0	95.6	35.6	29.3
16	Lawyers	8,980	44.5	17+	97.5	75.1	69.4	4.8
17	Judges	8,883	51.2	13.7	82.5	41.1	72.6	5.1
18	Computer systems analysts	8,852	29.7	14.9	93.3	43.4	80.6	13.9
19	College and university teachers, social science, nec.	8,843	39.7	17+	98.4	94.7	46.7	20.9
20	Industrial engineers	8,831	44.1	13.1	87.3	28.3	84.8	3.0
21	College and university teachers, economics	8,725	37.8	17+	99.9	95.6	36.4	8.6
22	Operations and systems researchers and analysts	8,473	39.2	14.0	99.1	36.0	81.5	24.5
23	Mathematicians	8,348	29.7	16.5	93.1	73.7	69.0	35.9
24	Psychologists	8,239	38.1	17+	98.5	89.0	42.9	
25	Railroad conductors	8,212	38.7	12.1	55.9		77.1	1.0
26	College and university teachers, psychology	8,076	36.6	17+	99.9	97.6	35.1	29.7
27	Vocational and educational counselors	8,063	41.0	17+	96.8	76.3	32.3	44.7
28	College and university teachers, health specialties	8,062	38.4	17+	97.0	76.7	43.4	47.4
29	Chemists	7,989	33.3	16.6	97.0	75.5	72.4	11.9
30	Managers and administrators, nec.—salaried: Durable goods manufacturing	7,949	46.7	12.7	81.3	16.5	83.7	3.5
31	School administrators, elementary and secondary	7,809	48.9	17+	94.8	76.8	42.4	26.9
32	Firemen, fire protection	7,769	39.0	12.4	71.6	2.5	76.7	1.3
33	Structural metal craftsmen	7,603	41.8	10.8	38.2		54.6	
34	College and university teachers, home economics	7,574	44.3	16.8	95.0	87.9	34.5	92.3
35	School administrators, college	7,537	45.4	16.0	95.4	65.5	65.4	23.0
36	Computer programers	7,453	26.6	12.7	98.1	50.9	68.6	22.9
37	Air traffic controllers		40.3		84.7	10.1	86.7	4.8
38	Managers and administrators, nec.—self-employed: Construction	7,349	46.3	12.4	63.8	14.5	66.7	1.4
39	College and university teachers, miscellaneous	7,316	36.8	17+	99.1	91.8	31.8	27.3

No.	Occupation	Ninth decile						
40	Sales managers, except retail trade	7,313	41.7	12.3	87.1	14.0	77.1	3.5
41	Computer specialists, nec.	7,277	33.3	12.9	94.9	30.0	76.2	13.2
42	Managers and administrators, nec.—salaried: Wholesale trade	7,258	47.9	12.7	79.4	11.5	78.3	4.6
43	Railroad and car shop mechanics	7,230	51.0	1.3	48.6		85.4	.9
44	Economists	7,228	35.2	16.1	95.9	53.5	67.8	11.5
45	Plumbers and pipefitters	7,205	43.2	1.7	47.4	.7	67.2	1.0
46	College and university teachers, coaches and physical education	7,188	32.1	17+	99.1	85.0	23.2	26.0
47	Managers and administrators, nec.—salaried services	7,174	40.4	12.7	87.3	16.3	83.6	10.7
48	Communications, utilities, and sanitary services	7,163	31.7	16.5	97.5	70.9	65.8	35.3
49	Biological scientists	7,149	49.4	12.5	93.6	30.4	81.4	44.8
50	Health administrators	7,118	39.1	14.1	93.2	36.3	74.5	40.3
51	Statisticians	7,071	47.1	12.3	89.2	17.9	81.1	18.8
52	Officials and administrators, public administration. nec	7,052	35.6	16.5	90.6	76.4	58.7	97.3
53	Home management advisors	7,050	32.0	17+	99.9	92.5	45.5	11.6
54	College and university teachers, chemistry	7,010	43.1	12.1	55.1	1.2	67.2	3.2
55	Aircraft mechanics	6,995	38.8	17.0	94.0	73.5	68.7	3.7
56	Architects	6,995	44.9	12.6	86.9	6.3	84.6	43.0
57	Clerical supervisors, nec.	6,975	34.8	16.8	99.1	93.0	20.9	48.4
58	Secondary school teachers, public	6,925	34.3	1.5	81.3		66.8	.9
59	Air conditioning, heating, and refrigeration mechanics	6,921	47.1	12.7	86.5	8.1	55.4	2.0
60	Officers, pilots, pursers, ship	6,889	45.2	12.7	98.6	86.3	83.7	13.7
61	Purchasing agents and buyers, nec.	6,883	38.5	16.5	99.5	94.8	20.5	83.6
62	Elementary schoolteachers, public	6,860	35.9	17+			26.9	41.8
63	College and university teachers, English — Managers and administrators, nec.—salaried: Nondurable goods manufacturing	6,847	46.3	12.5	74.5	16.1	79.1	6.2
64	Postmasters and mail superintendents	6,820	55.1	12.4	71.3	4.8	85.2	30.7
65	Farm management advisors	6,806	29.2	16.4	97.7	77.1	60.0	11.6
66	Cranemen, derrickmen, and hoistmen	6,734	42.0	10.9	41.6		53.8	1.3
67	Urban and regional planners	6,726	23.1	15.9	99.9	83.3	55.1	10.5
68	Tool programmers, numerical control	6,705	23.9	15.9	92.9	49.4	56.5	17.7
69	Managers and administrators, nec.—salaried: Business and repair services	6,695	41.6	12.9	85.3	19.6	76.3	11.5
70	Personnel and labor relations workers	6,681	41.2	12.9	89.3	24.3	73.2	31.5
71	Managers and administrators, nec.—salaried: Finance, insurance, real estate.	6,669	45.2	12.7	85.6	12.6	82.3	14.6
72	College and university teachers, business and commerce	6,654	38.3	17+	99.9	93.2	32.7	31.8
73	College and university teachers, sociology	6,631	33.4	17+	98.5	92.0	36.0	24.6
74	Telephone linemen and splicers	6,625	29.5	12.3	65.4		85.1	1.3
75	Railroad switchmen	6,609	38.6	12.3	66.0		64.2	1.9
76	Managers and administrators, nec.—salaried: All other industries.	6,604	45.8	14.0	86.7	36.6	69.0	20.1
77	Office managers, nec.	6,532	45.9	12.7	89.2	7.8	84.2	40.4
78	Social workers	6,475	37.1	16.4	93.6	66.2	64.2	62.9

Note: The extraordinarily high earnings for male dental hygienists, $14,291, compared with $5,704 for females, is probably the result of classification difficulties compounded by the small number of men (1,201) in the occupation. The classification includes hygienists in institutions such as mental hospitals and prisons. Some of these individuals may be dentists, causing a severe bias in the earnings data for male hygienists.

Source: Dixie Sommers, "Occupational Rankings for Men and Women by Earnings," Monthly Labor Review, U.S. Department of Labor, Bureau of Labor Statistics, August 1974, pp. 34-51. (Based on 1970 census data.)

TABLE 1.4

Selected Occupations of Men and Women, Ranked by 1969 Median Earnings, Bottom 20 Percent

Men

Rank	Occupation	Median annual earnings	Median age	Median school years completed	Percent completing 4 years of high school	Percent completing at least 4 years of college	Percent employed the full year	Percent of women in the occupation
Second decile								
338	Practical nurses	5,745	38.8	12.4	65.9	2.5	70.4	96.3
339	Barbers	5,686	45.5	11.4	44.8	.8	74.8	4.6
340	Freight and material handlers	5,660	33.2	10.9	39.3	1.1	60.4	7.4
341	Bartenders	5,656	46.3	12.0	50.6	3.8	66.2	21.4
342	Graders and sorters, manufacturing	5,635	38.1	10.5	37.0	1.3	65.6	68.1
343	Weavers	5,589	40.9	9.1	20.8	.2	77.1	53.6
344	Hucksters and peddlers	5,569	42.8	12.3	60.3	9.7	58.1	78.9
345	Farm service laborers, self-employed	5,566	44.6	11.4	45.0	1.2	59.7	15.1
346	Welfare service aides	5,487	34.9	12.7	71.8	25.4	65.2	76.0
347	Sales clerks, retail trade	5,482	35.5	12.4	63.3	6.8	64.7	65.2
348	Dyers	5,425	37.2	10.2	31.7	1.0	74.6	8.4
349	Clothing ironers and pressers	5,387	45.8	9.6	26.7	.5	63.0	74.5
350	Kindergarten teachers, private	5,382	33.9	14.4	74.9	39.1	50.5	98.4
351	Packers and wrappers, except meat and produce	5,336	32.3	10.9	38.6	1.1	61.5	62.5
352	Elevator operators	5,329	54.1	8.9	24.4	1.2	71.7	27.1
353	Counter clerks, except food	5,317	34.1	12.5	67.8	6.2	63.9	67.5
354	Duplicating machine operators	5,270	28.2	12.4	69.2	4.8	60.4	56.8
355	Office machine operators, nec	5,248	28.0	12.4	66.3	4.6	61.6	67.8
356	Construction laborers, except carpenters helpers	5,213	37.1	9.8	30.2	.9	46.9	1.7
357	Textile operatives, nec	5,184	37.6	9.7	27.6	.6	74.3	48.8
358	Taxicab drivers and chauffeurs	5,172	45.6	11.0	40.1	2.7	57.3	6.0
359	Sewers and stitchers	5,149	41.3	9.3	26.7	.9	59.1	93.8
360	Dressmakers and seamstresses, except factory	5,110	46.3	9.8	34.1	3.0	61.0	95.6
361	Spinners, twisters, and winders	5,078	33.7	9.5	26.2	.3	74.9	64.6
362	Shoe repairmen	5,070	52.6	8.9	28.4	.5	75.0	20.1
363	Kindergarten teachers, public	5,068	30.7	16.4	92.5	66.8	38.8	97.9
364	Shoemaking machine operatives	5,014	36.9	9.3	23.9	.4	70.3	62.0
365	Garbage collectors	4,981	37.6	9.3	23.8	.7	68.6	1.4
366	Teamsters	4,977	38.4	9.2	26.7	.6	49.0	3.8
367	Carding, lapping, and combing operatives	4,974	41.9	8.3	14.3	.5	77.6	26.1
368	Sawyers	4,972	41.4	9.0	26.3	.6	62.4	8.3
369	File clerks	4,952	27.6	12.5	72.7	6.6	56.4	82.1
370	Miscellaneous and not specified laborers	4,938	36.3	10.1	32.0	.8	57.7	10.8
371	Mail handlers, except post office	4,937	28.6	12.3	64.2	3.2	59.5	43.6
372	Laundry and drycleaning operatives, nec	4,830	42.7	10.6	36.0	1.4	67.2	63.3
373	Farmers, owners and tenants	4,816	51.0	10.7	42.9	3.5	85.8	4.8
374	Janitors and sextons	4,771	48.2	9.9	30.2	1.1	65.6	12.7
375	Chainmen, rodmen, and axmen, surveying	4,706	25.4	12.3	61.6	2.9	49.4	1.4
376	Musicians and composers	4,668	28.9	12.9	74.4	18.5	37.9	34.0
377	Fishermen and oystermen	4,623	40.9	9.5	27.9	1.6	45.3	4.1
378	Enumerators and interviewers	4,606	30.8	13.5	87.3	25.0	45.1	79.8
379	Dancers	4,421	29.0	12.9	77.7	23.2	38.7	81.6
380	Nursing aides, orderlies, and attendants	4,401	31.8	12.2	55.9	4.2	64.3	84.7

381	Health aides, except nursing	4,354	28.0	12.3	58.5	8.9	60.2	84.0
382	Receptionists	4,281	29.4	12.9	77.2	10.2	53.6	94.7
383	Boarding and lodging house keepers	4,256	56.1	12.2	54.1	10.5	79.9	73.9
384	Dental assistants	4,094	29.4	12.6	73.0	20.8	60.3	97.9
385	Cooks, except private household	4,076	31.3	10.9	36.7	1.4	52.6	62.5
386	Cleaners and charwomen	4,063	41.7	9.8	25.3	1.1	56.6	56.9
387	Attendants, personal service, nec	3,983	44.8	11.9	43.7	5.3	53.7	62.5
388	Animal caretakers, except farm	3,942	32.1	11.1	43.3	3.3	61.4	32.7
389	Child care workers, except private household	3,936	38.5	12.2	54.4	7.7	61.1	93.1
390	Lumbermen, raftsmen, and woodchoppers	3,835	37.0	8.8	23.3	.6	41.6	2.3
391	Gardeners and groundskeepers, except farm	3,792	42.8	9.7	23.6	1.6	51.5	3.0
392	Baggage porters and bellhops	3,746	36.8	11.7	45.4	3.2	54.6	2.2
393	Carpenters helpers	3,692	30.2	9.8	23.7	1.0	36.5	2.3
394	Vehicle washers and equipment cleaners	3,629	26.4	10.4	29.0	.7	49.3	10.8
395	Cooks, private household	3,552	54.0	9.8	30.4	2.7	67.7	94.2
396	Parking attendants	3,388	33.1	11.0	43.0	.7	51.0	3.2
397	Meat wrappers, retail trade	3,300	22.5	11.2	38.5	2.5	54.1	93.4
398	Chambermaids and maids, except private household	3,296	38.3	9.9	23.9	1.8	57.2	95.2
399	Cashiers	3,154	23.4	12.3	58.0	3.6	50.5	84.1
400	Housekeepers, private household	3,151	50.1	9.8	36.6	3.7	55.3	96.7
401	Messengers	3,029	28.9	11.4	43.8	2.9	46.3	20.9
402	Produce graders and sorters, except factory and farm	2,959	38.4	8.9	23.9	.8	38.6	75.5
403	Waiters	2,894	27.7	11.7	47.2	3.7	40.6	89.2
404	Garage workers and gas station attendants	2,668	22.0	11.1	25.8	.9	44.3	2.8
405	Crossing guards and bridgetenders	2,620	64.5	9.1	27.3	1.2	42.8	59.3
406	Laundresses, private household	2,596	54.9	10.0	34.3	4.2	67.8	95.8
407	Farm laborers, wage workers	2,493	36.7	8.7	21.9	.8	51.4	14.3
408	Health trainees	2,413	22.9	12.5	61.1	12.4	48.8	93.9
409	Stock handlers	2,114	19.5	11.3	38.5	.9	43.3	17.6
410	Attendants, recreation and amusement	1,923	23.9	12.0	49.8	3.6	36.4	24.5
411	Food service workers, n.e.c., except private household	1,917	21.9	10.8	22.7	1.5	37.3	75.5
412	Teacher aides, except school monitors	1,769	23.0	13.6	28.2	18.9	24.4	89.6
413	Maids and servants, private household	1,631	48.6	8.9	21.2	1.5	49.2	96.6
414	Library attendants and assistants	1,546	21.9	13.9	29.8	19.1	31.0	78.8
415	Food counter and fountain workers	1,413	19.2	11.1	25.6	1.1	30.9	76.0
416	Dishwashers	1,238	19.4	10.5	26.3	.9	25.7	37.8
417	Bootblacks	1,176	52.6	8.2	44.5	.8	47.8	8.3
418	School monitors	1,153	21.3	12.9	46.9	7.6	28.2	91.0
419	Farm laborers, unpaid family workers	1,100	20.3	10.8	24.0	1.4	63.4	41.3
420	Busboys	943	17.9	10.8	24.0	.9	20.6	14.1
421	Ushers, recreation and amusement	895	17.9	11.0	29.0	2.2	17.8	31.2
422	Newsboys	795	17.7	10.7	30.7	1.8	60.1	16.1
423	Child care workers, private household	687	19.8	10.6	34.1	.4	21.5	98.0

(continued)

19

(Table 1.4 continued)

Women

Rank	Occupation	Median annual earnings	Median age	Median school years completed	Percent completing at least 4 years of high school	Percent completing at least 4 years of college	Percent employed the full year	Percent of women in the occupation
Second decile								
313	Graders and sorters, manufacturing	3,103	43.1	10.2	30.7	.2	40.0	68.1
314	Salesmen, retail trade	3,092	44.8	12.3	64.3	3.9	54.9	13.0
315	Elevator operators	3,071	46.4	10.7	34.2	.7	61.6	27.1
316	Hairdressers and cosmetologists	3,041	33.3	12.3	66.2	.4	52.9	90.1
317	Clergymen	3,020	48.0	13.3	76.8	33.6	73.6	2.9
318	Bartenders	3,008	41.5	11.6	45.2	.8	55.7	21.4
319	Clothing ironers and pressers	2,980	43.6	9.7	24.6	.2	56.9	74.5
320	Nursing aides, orderlies and attendants	2,969	38.1	11.8	47.7	.7	53.7	84.7
321	Radio and television announcers	2,963	37.9	13.4	91.4	27.4	52.9	6.4
322	Managers and superintendents, building	2,942	52.6	12.3	60.2	6.8	70.5	40.8
323	Miscellaneous and not specified laborers	2,942	39.5	10.4	34.1	.9	44.5	10.8
324	Counter clerks, except food	2,938	38.2	12.3	62.5	1.8	51.9	67.5
325	Decorators and window dressers	2,923	42.7	12.5	70.1	7.1	52.6	58.5
326	Boarding and lodging housekeepers	2,852	58.9	12.1	42.5	3.9	81.1	73.9
327	Deliverymen and routemen	2,844	37.0	12.0	50.0	1.8	48.8	3.2
328	Vehicle washers and equipment cleaners	2,801	36.4	10.1	26.0	.7	44.3	10.8
329	Bakers	2,798	48.5	11.1	40.5	.5	44.9	29.5
330	Laundry and drycleaning operatives, nec.	2,789	45.5	10.0	28.2	.4	57.7	63.3
331	Stock handlers	2,755	37.7	11.5	44.3		50.9	17.6
332	Carpenters helpers	2,746	29.6	10.7	37.6		39.1	2.3
333	Farm managers	2,744	48.5	12.2	56.7	7.1	72.6	4.1
334	Taxicab drivers and chauffeurs	2,702	42.0	11.7	46.8	1.3	40.9	6.0
335	Farm service laborers, self-employed	2,679	44.9	11.6	45.2	10.3	40.3	15.1
336	Dressmakers and seamstresses, except factory	2,664	53.6	10.8	40.0	1.8	50.0	95.6
337	Bottling and canning operatives	2,626	43.5	10.0	28.5	.2	30.7	40.0
338	Lay midwives	2,626	43.4	12.3	63.4	2.2	53.0	76.5
339	Lumbermen, raftsmen, and woodchoppers	2,605	40.4	10.0	28.4	3.0	48.0	2.3
340	Attendants, personal service, nec.	2,576	42.7	12.1	54.1	4.7	40.2	62.5
341	Surveyors	2,510	36.8	12.6	76.1	9.1	40.3	3.4
342	Recreation workers	2,476	29.0	13.7	83.0	26.1	41.7	41.7
343	College and university teachers, atmospheric, earth, marine, and space	2,471	24.9	17+	99.9	87.7	30.4	11.4
344	Parking attendants	2,458	37.8	11.3	41.3	4.0	28.3	3.2
345	Cleaners and charwomen	2,445	48.1	9.4	22.8	.4	56.3	56.9
346	Cashiers	2,431	32.9	12.1	56.7	1.0	45.0	84.1
347	Religious workers, nec.	2,405	46.8	14.7	88.7	39.9	59.6	55.7
348	Janitors and sextons	2,404	48.9	9.8	27.9	.8	56.6	12.7
349	Sign painters and letterers	2,315	28.8	12.2	57.7	4.0	51.5	9.2
350	Salesmen of services and construction	2,256	37.0	12.3	63.7	5.4	42.7	35.1
351	Garage workers and gas station attendants	2,241	29.4	11.1	37.1	1.0	46.9	2.8

Bottom decile	Occupation							
352	Sales clerks, retail trade	2,208	43.2	12.2	55.7	2.0	46.7	65.2
353	Farmers, owners and tenants	2,173	51.0	11.4	46.2	4.2	78.6	4.8
354	Cooks, except private household	2,157	48.1	10.5	31.8	.4	40.4	62.5
355	Messengers	2,110	31.2	12.3	61.1	2.1	39.3	20.9
356	Animal caretakers, except farm	2,060	29.8	13.1	58.5	3.1	44.5	32.7
357	Library attendants and assistants	2,058	44.9	9.7	81.2	18.5	41.3	78.8
358	Chambermaids and maids, except private household	2,048	44.6	9.6	24.8	.5	46.7	95.2
359	Produce graders and packers, except factory and farm	1,982	41.3	14.5	22.7	.8	22.3	75.5
360	Teachers, except college and university nec	1,936	38.1	14.4	81.7	37.5	30.2	70.4
361	Kindergarten teachers, private	1,898	43.5	14.4	85.6	33.9	19.1	98.4
362	Gardeners and groundskeepers, except farm	1,875	39.2	12.1	38.5	1.9	38.7	3.0
363	Busdrivers	1,862	38.7	10.0	55.0	.6	12.1	28.4
364	Fishermen and oystermen	1,842	44.0	10.9	28.9	1.1	35.5	4.1
365	Food service workers, nec, except private household	1,839	37.3	12.6	31.1	.5	33.6	75.5
366	Teacher aides, except school monitors	1,672	23.6	12.9	80.7	5.0	12.9	89.6
367	Motion picture projectionists	1,669	31.6	12.9	86.5	7.3	37.7	3.8
368	Waitresses	1,662	27.9	11.5	45.2	.9	34.8	89.2
369	Athletes and kindred workers	1,650	55.2	12.9	77.9	17.5	28.4	28.3
370	Cooks, private household	1,599	38.6	8.7	18.6	.5	58.1	94.2
371	Newsboys	1,529	44.1	12.0	51.1	1.2	55.4	16.1
372	Crossing guards and bridgetenders	1,494	39.1	12.0	55.0	.7	9.4	59.3
373	Enumerators and interviewers	1,460	37.5	12.7	81.0	11.7	22.8	79.8
374	Musicians and composers	1,395	35.1	13.6	84.5	27.4	38.6	34.0
375	Food counter and fountain workers	1,382	40.7	11.5	45.1	.7	25.6	76.0
376	Child care workers, except private household	1,375	53.1	12.0	53.2	3.7	37.5	93.1
377	Paperhangers	1,330	53.5	11.6	46.3	3.5	21.3	10.1
378	Housekeepers, private household	1,318	35.1	8.9	22.6	.6	51.3	96.7
379	Demonstrators	1,266	40.2	12.4	71.7	4.4	26.0	90.8
380	Dishwashers	1,235	51.2	10.0	26.6	.2	32.0	37.8
381	Maids and servants, private household	1,093	37.5	8.8	18.5	.6	45.3	96.6
382	Farm laborers, wage workers	992	23.4	8.9	21.1	.8	24.2	14.3
383	Attendants, recreation and amusement	979	39.0	12.2	55.2	3.1	26.9	24.5
384	Hucksters and peddlers	956	19.8	12.3	62.0	3.2	32.0	78.9
385	Busboys	925	21.8	10.9	31.4	.6	22.2	14.1
386	Health trainees	871	19.0	13.4	90.4	4.1	17.0	93.9
387	Ushers, recreation and amusement	781	44.5	11.9	48.8	4.3	15.9	31.2
388	Farm laborers, unpaid family workers	768	56.0	12.0	55.5	1.3	77.4	41.3
389	Laundresses, private household	756	32.1	8.7	18.8	1.0	50.4	95.8
390	Child care workers, private household	671	40.0	10.7	35.7	1.4	21.6	98.0
391	School monitors	647			70.7	3.6	7.5	91.0

Source: Dixie Sommers, "Occupational Rankings for Men and Women by Earnings," Monthly Labor Review, U.S. Department of Labor, Bureau of Labor Statistics, August 1974, pp. 34-51. (Based on 1970 census data.)

FIGURE 1.2

Underrepresentation of Women as Managers and Skilled Craft Workers

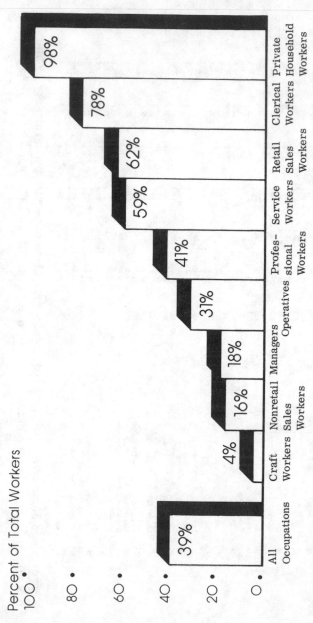

*Among professional workers, the 1970 census showed women as 9 percent of physicians, 5 percent of lawyers, while representing 84 percent of public elementary school teachers and 97 percent of registered nurses. (See Tables 1.3 and 1.4 for earnings.)

Source: Prepared by the Women's Bureau, Employment Standards Administration, from 1974 annual averages data published by the Bureau of Labor Statistics, U.S. Department of Labor.

Girls and young women are indeed "being held back" because they have less access to the universities, colleges, trade schools, federally sponsored training and apprentice programs that are the main routes to satisfying lifetime employment. The result of women's lower representation in postsecondary education is shown in Tables 1.2, 1.3, and 1.4, and Figure 1.2. Women are only a small percentage of the top-paid professions and skilled trades-- doctor, lawyer, machinist--and a high percentage of clerical, sales, and domestic employment.

The educational institutions where women are generally least-well-represented are at the same time the institutions receiving the greatest support from taxpayers. The top 100 higher education institutions received two-thirds of the $4 billion federal obligations in fiscal year 1973; the share of these major institutions in fact increased slightly over fiscal year 1972 levels, so that the comparative faculty, research, and facilities of these institutions are further enhanced relative to the less prestigious institutions where women are a higher percent of enrollment.[20] Tax exemptions to corporate and foundation donors also subsidize the major private universities where women undergraduates are outnumbered by about 3:2. These "research universities," which represent only 7 percent of all institutions, in 1973-74 received 40 percent of the almost $1 billion of support from these private donors.[21] State tax-fund appropriations also typically favor the research universities and associated medical facilities where women are generally least-well-represented in each state.[22] Direct funding in fiscal year 1974 of $853 million from federal, state, and local taxes of postsecondary vocational school programs benefited about 3 men for every 2 women in public noncollegiate postsecondary institutions.[23] Almost $400 million in federal funds for institutional and on-the-job training programs likewise was directed to more than three times as many men as women in 1974 programs.[24] Thus in the U.S. educational system beyond high school, young women are not receiving equal opportunity with young men for more rewarding lifetime careers, yet they and their tax-paying parents are sharing in the costs of these programs.

OUTLINE OF THE STUDY

What can explain this denial of opportunity to half our youthful population? We will seek to explore in the following chapters the extent of this discrimination and to explain why this discriminatory pattern has been perpetuated by educators long after woman's life role has changed substantially.

In Chapter 2 we will look at sex discrimination in the education system nationwide, and in Chapter 3 will look more closely at educational opportunities for women in each of 20 states. These include the ten largest states in population, five middle-sized, and five small states, scattered geographically. This state-by-state analysis will permit young women to assess their chances for vocational and academic education in their home states and at the "national" universities and professional schools as well. Then if a young woman in Florida, New Jersey, or Wyoming becomes aware that she is being denied equal educational opportunity in institutions supported by her parents' taxes, she will be able to take appropriate action (for example, by using the new Title IX of the Higher Education Act, see Appendix A) to open up the education system.

In Chapter 4 we will seek an economic rationale for the persistence of sex-discriminatory admissions policies. Using that understanding, Chapter 5 will suggest ways in which young women and their parents can achieve equal educational opportunities in each state. As more than half the eligible voters, women can elect state and federal officials committed to equal admission standards, fairly administered, to the institutions that control access to career opportunities.

It should be noted here that there are other important areas of discrimination in educational opportunity that will not be discussed in this study, simply because it is not possible to do justice to all aspects of unequal educational opportunity in one study. The problem of unequal access to education and training opportunities for young men of minority races has been documented and discussed elsewhere (though it has not been solved). Likewise, the problem of the older woman who is married and seeking to remedy educational deficiencies while at the same time maintaining home and family is now being given more attention in studies of continuing education.

There is not space to discuss these serious and persistent problems in the present study, yet an effective restructuring of American education beyond high school will benefit all those now denied opportunities to develop their full talents. Sexism and racism in education are closely related, both serving to perpetuate the status quo in employment opportunities throughout life. This book, then, will focus on the lack of educational opportunity for all young women-- whether black, white, Asian, Chicana, Puerto Rican, or any other race, creed, or nationality--in the education system of the United States.

NOTES

1. Ellen Goodman, "A Girl Fights for Her Rights," Boston Evening Globe, July 9, 1974, p. 15.

2. U.S. Department of Labor, Years for Decision, Vol. II, Manpower Research Monograph No. 24 (Washington, D.C., 1974).

3. U.S. Department of Labor, Women's Bureau, The Earnings Gap (Washington, D.C., March 1975); Eileen Shanahan, New York Times, July 6, 1974, p. 1.

4. U.S. Department of Labor, Women's Bureau, Women's Handbook (Washington, D.C., 1969), Table 1, p. 10; U.S. Working Women: A Chartbook (Washington, D.C., 1975), Chart 2.

5. U.S. Department of Commerce, Bureau of the Census, Characteristics of American Youth, 1974, C.P.R. Special Studies, Ser. P23, No. 51.

6. Gloria Stevenson, "Career Planning for High School Girls," Occupational Outlook Quarterly, Summer 1973, pp. 23-31.

7. U.S. Department of Labor, "Urban Family Budget Updated to Autumn 1974," Monthly Labor Review, June 1975, pp. 42-48.

8. Patricia Cross, Beyond the Open Door (San Francisco: Jossey-Bass, 1971), quoting A. Anastasi, Differential Psychology, rev. ed. (New York: Macmillan, 1958), pp. 660-63.

9. Carnegie Commission on Higher Education, Opportunities for Women in Higher Education (New York: McGraw-Hill, 1973), p. 272.

10. College Entrance Examination Board, College-Bound Seniors, 1973-74 (Evanston, Ill.: CEEB, 1974), Table 3, p. 18.

11. Ibid., Table 4, p. 18; p. 8.

12. Education Commission of the States, National Assessment of Educational Progress: Citizenship, 1971; Reading, 1972; Science, 1970; Writing, 1971 (Denver, 1971-72).

13. U.S. Department of Labor, Bureau of Apprenticeship Training, Women in Apprenticeship (Washington, D.C., August 1970), pp. 1-6.

14. U.S. Office of Civil Rights, Preliminary report, enrollment in public postsecondary area vocational schools, January 1974 (U.S. Department of Health, Education, and Welfare draft bulletin, March 1976).

15. U.S. Department of Health, Education, and Welfare, National Center for Educational Statistics, draft of preliminary report, 1973-74 enrollment noncollegiate postsecondary schools with occupational programs (Washington, D.C., March 1976).

16. O. R. Perry, B. E. Anderson, R. L. Rowan, and H. R. Northrup, The Impact of Government Manpower Programs in General and on Minorities and Women (Philadelphia: University of Pennsylvania, Wharton School, 1975), p. 24.

17. U.S. Department of Labor, Manpower Report of the President, 1974 (Washington, D.C., 1974), pp. 133-34.

18. U.S. Department of Health, Education, and Welfare, Vocational and Technical Education 1969 (Washington, D.C., 1970), Table 7, p. 39.

19. U.S. Department of Labor, Manpower Report of the President, 1975 (Washington, D.C., 1975), Table F-4, p. 321.

20. National Science Foundation, Federal Support to Universities, Colleges and Selected Nonprofit Institutions, FY 1973 (Washington, D.C., 1975), p. ix.

21. Council for Financial Aid to Education, Survey of Voluntary Support of Education 1973-74 (New York, 1975), pp. 5-6.

22. Council for Financial Aid to Education, Handbook of Aid to Higher Education (New York, 1972), Tables D-1 to D-50.

23. U.S. Department of Health, Education, and Welfare, Vocational and Technical Education, FY 1974, Vocational Education Information III, Table 008, p. 6.

24. U.S. Department of Labor, Manpower Report of the President, 1975, op. cit., Table F-2, p. 318.

2

EXPLANATIONS OF WOMEN'S MINORITY STATUS IN POSTSECONDARY EDUCATION

As we indicated in Chapter 1, girls do better than boys with respect to school grades, from kindergarten through college. Why then should young women be a decided minority in top-ranking colleges and universities as well as in professional and vocational training? One answer could be that young women themselves do not seek admission to these schools for a variety of reasons: lack of self-confidence; discouragement by parents and guidance counselors; inappropriate high school programs; lack of funds; ignorance of opportunities; or for a number of other reasons. In the first part of this chapter we will explore the possible reasons for the smaller number of women in postsecondary education from the standpoint of aspiration of young women. In the second part we will look at the problem from the other side. Do young women in fact seek admission to these institutions and occupational programs, only to be denied admission by discriminatory practices of public and private colleges and universities, public vocational schools, government agencies, or labor unions?

SOME REASONS WHY WOMEN ARE A MINORITY IN POSTSECONDARY EDUCATION

Is it her own hand that holds a woman back? If so, why? Some evidence indicates that bright young women do not apply to all institutions of higher education in equal numbers with young men. In 1974, for example, there were 7,800 male applicants to Harvard, but only 3,400 women applied to Radcliffe. [1] In view of girls' better school grades, why should this be so? Some possible reasons are listed below.

The Put-Down of Girls in School Texts

There is not enough space and probably little need to detail all
the ways in which women have been taught to belittle their own intel-
ligence and abilities. "Dick and Jane as Victims" is one of the first
and most thoroughly documented studies of school texts. Little girls
have been and are being taught through texts in use from coast to
coast,[2]

that girls are not as bright as boys	"It's easy. Even I can do it. And you know how stupid I am. " (spoken by a girl)
nor as brave	"Oh Raymond, boys are much braver than girls. " (a girl)
nor as resolute	"She is just like a girl. She gives up. " (a boy)
nor as capable	"A woman driving her car does not stop at a corner. She runs into a truck. " (the text)
nor as worthy	"She's almost as good as a real boy. " (a boy)

Girls are also taught through the use of such texts that they are
physical weaklings, always pictured passively watching while boys
play or climb or build; that the only occupations open to women are
as mother, nurse, teacher, or office worker. Few women are pictured even driving a car, while the same school texts show men as
engineers, doctors, mechanics.

The Need for Parental Encouragement

Parents, although loving sons and daughters equally, apparently have different aspirations for children depending on their sex.
In one study of high school seniors, 47 percent of boys but only 37
percent of girls reported that their fathers "definitely desired" college for them; for mothers, it was 49 percent for boys, but again
37 percent for girls.[3] These parents are products of the same educational system described above, which taught them that human
beings of the female sex have less need for education beyond high
school. In an interesting experiment set up to determine whether
women value other women, psychologist Philip Goldberg made a

collection of articles in the fields of law, city plannings, nutrition, and other specialized areas. These articles were bound into two sets--in one set a particular article would be identified as written by John Brown; in the other set, the same article would be identified as written by Jane Brown, and similarly for the other articles. When the class of women students was divided into two groups and asked to evaluate each article on style and content, the articles attributed to male authors scored significantly higher.[4] Even other women assume that studies produced by women are for that reason of less value. Thus it is not surprising that more mothers would like to see their sons enter college than have that ambition for their daughters.

Studies indicate that the greatest influence on whether students went to college was exercised by parents and peers.[5] Since parents have lower educational aspirations for their daughters, and the daughters' peers in the teen years include mainly other girls, it might be expected that fewer girls than boys would aspire to college and even fewer to top universities.

Financial Problems

A series of studies, the latest referring to 1967, revealed that only 60 percent of the brightest girls in the poorest socioeconomic quarter were attending college, as compared to 75 percent of the high-ability boys in the same financial circumstances. Fewer girls than boys at every level of ability went on to college in this low-income group. Only in the top socioeconomic quarter did as high a percent of girls go on to college[6] (see Table 2.1).

Counseling

The attitudes of high school guidance counselors in many cases also discourages young women from entering studies leading to non-traditional fields. Overworked guidance counselors, assigned impossibly high numbers of students, can not thoroughly explore all fields with each student. However, a questionnaire sent out in 1972 by the Massachusetts Governor's Commission on the Status of Women asked guidance counselors whether there was a difference in the counseling given boys and girls. Almost one-third answered that there was a difference, and one responded, "I am biased toward the girl becoming a housewife, although I would like her to have a saleable skill."[7] Such counseling leads to enrollment in brief skill-training programs designed for short-term employment before

TABLE 2.1

High School Graduates Attending Two- or Four-Year Colleges,
by Socioeconomic Class and Sex
(in percent)

	Socioeconomic Quarter											
	1 (low)			2			3			4 (high)		
Ability Quarter	1957[a]	1961[b]	1967[c]	1957	1961	1967	1957	1961	1967	1957	1961	1967
Male												
1 (low)	6	9	33	12	14	30	18	16	29	39	34	57
2	17	16	43	27	25	39	34	36	55	61	45	61
3	28	32	60	43	38	69	51	48	68	73	72	79
4 (high)	52	58	75	59	74	80	72	79	89	91	90	92
Female												
1 (low)	4	8	25	9	12	28	16	13	36	33	26	37
2	6	13	28	20	12	36	26	21	50	44	37	67
3	9	25	44	24	30	48	31	40	68	67	65	77
4 (high)	28	34	60	37	51	73	48	71	83	76	85	93

[a]1957 graduates, with 1964 follow-up.
[b]1961 graduates, with 1962 follow-up.
[c]1967 graduates, with 1968 follow-up.

Source: Patricia Cross, Beyond the Open Door (San Francisco: Jossey-Bass, 1971), Table 1.

marriage, but not to the acquisition of knowledge and skills for a
lifetime of paid employment.

Public School Authority Structure

Most principals, superintendents, and department heads are
men; most classroom teachers are women. In 1970-71 women were
67 percent of classroom teachers, but less than 21 percent of elementary school principals, 3 percent of high school principals, and
only 1 percent of superintendents. [8] The young girl internalizes the
role of women as subordinates, and she sees few role-models to
persuade her that women have the scholarly or executive ability necessary for leadership.

Course Structure

The persistence of outmoded "tracks" for the two sexes creates
two different study programs in most public high schools. In the
words of one guidance counselor, in the same Massachusetts study
cited above, "Physics is assumed to be a subject for boys--biology
for girls."[9] Although the girls who do take additional math courses
do better than boys gradewise (64 percent of girls and 63 percent of
boys had As and Bs in high school mathematics),[10] only 8 percent of
girls reported at least four years of high school math, compared to
57 percent of boys, in an earlier Berkeley study.* As a result,
"Without a fourth year of high school math, it is impossible at U.C.
[University of California] Berkeley to enter engineering, computer
science, economics, business, mathematics or any of the sciences.
Thus, females are effectively excluded from many fields before they
enter the university."[11] Quite simply, the game is over, and lost,
before the majority of high school girls have heard of the rules.
There are fewer girls than boys inspired or qualified to apply to the
top technical schools such as MIT or Cal Tech--and women's lower
average scores on the mathematics portion of the SAT test are quite
simply accounted for.

In vocational programs associated with high schools, administrators, often in violation of state law as well as of federal Title IX

---

*This ratio has risen in recent years; the 1974 ATP program
questionnaire shows 37 percent of girls, 59 percent of boys reporting four or more years of high school math (see College Entrance
Examination Board, College-Bound Seniors, 1973-74 [Evanston, Ill.:
CEEB, 1974], Table 4).

(see Appendix A), restrict girls to "women's fields"--typing, child care--so that girls have no opportunity to discover and develop interests and skills in woodworking, metalworking, and the like, and thus once again are barred from entrance to vocational programs beyond high school because they lack the background needed for passing "aptitude" tests. Project Talent reported that less than 10 percent of girls but more than 30 percent of boys had three or more vocational courses. [12]

Denial of Training in Organized Sports

Girls have been denied opportunity for developing skills and self-confidence through sports activities of public schools, although Title IX may now move school authorities toward correction of gross inequities. The Massachusetts study indicated that the ratio of public school sports expenditures for boys relative to girls ran as high as 100:1, and studies in Michigan, Texas, Minnesota, and other states also found wide disparity. [13] Young women are not merely being denied physical development, important though that is; they are being denied training in self-discipline, sportsmanship, and cooperation, as well as the sense of unmistakable achievement that organized sports provide.

It appears then that the seeds of self-doubt and low aspiration are nurtured in the young girl by parental attitudes, school texts, courses of study, athletic programs, and male authority structure of the public school system. We cannot doubt that these factors play some part in limiting the aspiration of young women to top-ranked colleges and universities, as well as to vocational schools.

It should be noted at this point that young women today are beginning to question the sex-stereotyped education they have received from kindergarten through high school. In a 1973 YWCA study in four cities (El Paso, Tex.; Greenfield, S.C.; Philadelphia, Pa.; and South Bend, Ind.) 81 percent of teen-agers listed "help in finding jobs" as the most needed service. Job training ranked in top place among all racial and ethnic groups. "The teen women said that preparation for jobs does not come early enough, clearly enough, or fairly," adding such comments as:

> "We need to know how to do something else besides
>   cleaning house."
> "We need training for a wider variety of jobs."
> "Why aren't girls trained to do anything outside the
>   house besides office work?"
> "Girls usually don't get any training except for sec-
>   retarial or teaching jobs." [14]

Yet the lower aspiration levels of young women persist, as reflected
in the report of the College Entrance Examination Board (CEEB),
covering about 1 million 1973-74 high school seniors taking the
Scholastic Aptitude Test. Twice as many females as males planned
only a two-year degree while more than twice as many males as
females planned to complete M.D., Ph.D., or other professional
degrees. The most frequently reported intended fields for women in
the CEEB study were education, nursing, and biological sciences,
while for men biological sciences (pre-med), business, engineering,
and social sciences were cited. [15]

Granting then that the reported lower career aspirations of
young women, derived from influences described in the previous
pages, play some part in the numerical superiority of young men in
education beyond high school, we must still investigate this fundamental question: For those young women with the requisite ability
and aspirations, is there equal opportunity for admission to such
educational institutions, academic and vocational?

SOME DISCRIMINATORY ADMISSIONS POLICIES

In the first part of this chapter we presented evidence that
some young women may be held back in achieving higher education
and professional or vocational training by their own lack of aspiration. But this does not exclude the other possibility: that women
are denied admission to higher education and vocational training by
discriminatory practices of public and private colleges and universities, public vocational schools, government agencies, or labor
unions. Alice de Rivera, a teen-ager who sought to open up the
sex-segregated science high schools of New York City a few years
back, wrote of the "dark space" in her mind with "no real plans for
the future"; yet when she became interested in a career in science,
she found out that girls were not admitted to the specialized public
high school of science. [16]

As the YWCA study indicated, other young women have begun
to recognize those "dark spaces" and have become aware that, for
all but unskilled jobs, education and training are a necessity. The
question we will explore in this section is simply: Is someone
standing in the schoolhouse door?

We will look in turn at (1) the public and private (nonprofit)
postsecondary academic institutions, and (2) the public vocational
programs, for evidence of sex-discriminatory admissions policies
(including financial aid). We will focus on public vocational institutions because of the obvious interest of taxpayers in institutions
directly supported from public funds. There is, moreover, considerable variation in the quality and reliability of proprietary

(for-profit) vocational institutions, as well as a lack of good data on numbers enrolled, graduates, and the like.[17] In general, private proprietary vocational enrollments are similar to those of the public postsecondary sector--young men the majority in technical, trades, and industry fields, young women predominant in office and health programs.

Types of Postsecondary Institutions

It is worth spending a little time to describe the possible post-secondary educational alternatives, because the typical teen-age girl has only limited information of the possibilities of education and employment beyond high school. Her parents, generally 40 to 60 years of age, are unlikely themselves to have attended college; less than one-third of whites in this age bracket have had any college experience, and for blacks the percentage is even lower.[18] Only 28 percent of all men and 22 percent of all women over 18 were reported in the 1970 census as having completed vocational training.[19] Thus, given the lack of knowledge of the average high schooler and her parents, coupled with the impossibly high work load of high school guidance counselors, the move from high school to further education is made on the basis of very limited information. The brief summary below is intended to fill that gap, looking in turn at two-year colleges, four-year colleges and universities providing academic degree programs; and then examining vocational institutions of various types.

Two-Year Community or Junior Colleges

Two-year colleges generally offer both degree-credit (college-parallel) programs, permitting transfer after two years to advanced standing at a four-year institution, and terminal-occupational programs, of varying duration, providing occupational skills in mechanical, electrical, technical, health, office, or other fields. We will discuss the degree-credit programs here under Academic Programs, and the terminal-occupational courses under Vocational Programs.

Two-year colleges are the newest and fastest growing of the academic institutions. Although 75 percent of entering students declare their intention to transfer to a four-year college after completion of two years, less than 35 percent actually do transfer.[20] The two-year degree program has been described by sociologists as a "cooling out" process, in which unrealistic aspirations of students

are brought down to earth by actual experience of college study requirements.

The faculty in two-year colleges are often highly qualified.
This is particularly true of women, who may have received Ph.D.
degrees from top-level universities but find themselves rejected for
employment by these same institutions, or others of comparable
quality. However, the facilities tend to be quite limited, especially
with respect to libraries and laboratories. This limitation may restrict those students who do transfer to a lower rank of four-year
institution, with less chance of admission to universities for advanced
study. Therefore it is important that high school students of the
requisite high academic ability recognize that some institutions provide better access than others to professional and scientific careers.

Four-Year Institutions
(Universities and Colleges)

A university generally includes, in addition to an undergraduate
college of arts and sciences, a number of professional schools, at
undergraduate or graduate levels--for example, business, law,
medicine, education, nursing, social work. Among the over 2,500
institutions of higher education in the United States, only a few hundred regularly grant significant numbers of doctoral and professional
degrees.

To begin at the top, some universities, frequently described
as "major," or "national" universities, have been described by the
Carnegie Commission as "Research Universities" (see Appendix C).
These schools attract students and faculty from all areas of this
country and abroad. Because of their reputation, these schools attract substantial funds from alumni and other private donors, as
well as foundation grants and federal research contracts. Such comparative affluence permits these universities to attract, support,
and retain on the faculty research scholars of Nobel Prize-winning
stature, and to offer scholarships and other financial aid to the most
promising of each year's crop of high school graduates, identified
by high SAT scores, National Merit awards, school or athletic leadership records, or similar distinction. These schools have many
more freshman applicants than they can admit, and therefore can be
highly selective in their admissions policies.

Less-well-known universities, categorized by the Carnegie
Commission as "comprehensive universities," are more likely to
encompass undergraduate schools of education, business, or nursing. Partly because these schools have smaller budget appropriations (if public) or endowments (if private) they attract fewer of the
outstanding students and faculty; in circular fashion, this then

worsens their financial problems by perpetuating lower levels of
support from public funds or from private donors. Such financial
limitations restrict the possibility of extensive research activity to
attract top faculty, or of scholarship aid, to draw top students. Some
of the institutions in this classification have been teacher-training
institutions with a high proportion of women students.

Liberal arts colleges vary in quality. Although most are co-
educational, some outstanding liberal arts colleges admit only
women, while others of equally high quality admit only men.* Many
private liberal arts colleges have a history of financial problems;
this factor, as well as small enrollments, makes it more difficult
for them to attract and retain top faculty, to compete for substantial
research grants, and to provide broad financial aid to students.
Women's colleges admit less than 10 percent of all women undergraduates and have generally small or medium enrollments.

Because the declining birth rate is lowering enrollments in
public schools, many state colleges that have been oriented to
"teacher training" have begun to emphasize liberal arts, or, as
noted above, have moved to become "comprehensive universities."

Research Universities

Thus, with no reflection on the quality, dedication, and ability
of faculty across the spectrum of higher education, it must be recognized that the "national," "research" universities are best equipped
to engage in the competition for talent among each successive high
school graduating class. Talent is scarce. In baseball or in education, "expansion teams" have difficulty making the grade, because
of the scarcity of resources. Not only would it be prohibitively
costly to duplicate the physical facilities of Harvard, MIT, or
Berkeley, with respect to libraries, laboratories, and other physical
plant; it probably would be impossible to provide an equivalent group
of faculty and researchers to such an institution. Most fundamental
of all, the pool of top-level high school graduates is likewise finite.
This may have been the concern that led Rockefeller, Carnegie, and
other early donors to the field of education, to support only those
few institutions that seemed capable of achieving scholarly eminence.

This is not the place to debate the virtues of such shaping of
the American higher education system by private philanthropy. Much
can be said pro and con, and the subject is well discussed by Curti
and Nash.[21] For the present purposes, it is enough to point out that

---

*The number of single-sex schools has declined sharply in the
past decade.

by 1920, "twenty institutions had received about 75 percent of all foundation philanthropy."[22] For good or ill, today we have a system of higher education in which certain institutions of higher education --whether by virtue of past donations, legislative action, intelligent management, or any other cause--receive the vast bulk of endowment income, federal research contracts, and private foundation grants. These institutions are therefore able to support a highly rated faculty, expensive library and laboratory facilities, and thus to enjoy the merited prestige that attracts great numbers of freshmen applicants, even in the face of relatively high tuition charges. These differences in funds, faculty, and facilities among the several thousand institutions of higher education are of crucial importance in opening career opportunities for undergraduate students.

At a 1972 conference on the Benefits of Higher Education, the panelists expressed in discussion ("more openly than in the papers") a general dissatisfaction with the use of "years of schooling" to measure the effect of different kinds of education beyond high school on the subsequent life experience and income of individuals. "The measure is imperfect because it implies that an education at Princeton and Podunk are the same thing."[23] Thus educators clearly recognize, as young women and their parents often do not, that a college education may vary among institutions in acceptability to business firms, government agencies, and admission officials of law, medical, and other professional schools.

Society has a great stake in the education of each youthful generation. Education is costly, yet as "investment in human capital," such use of economic resources ultimately brings high returns.* Greater productivity of business enterprises, as well as scientific breakthroughs in the fields of health and energy technology, have flowed out of university research. In order to maximize returns, however, we cannot exclude some of our high-potential youth from the selection process. This has been the case with respect to women.

Restricted Access to Tax-Supported "Research Universities"

As the preceding discussion suggests, discrimination against women is demonstrated not just by women's lower percentage of the total undergraduate enrollment, but by women's low percentage in many of the top-ranked research universities (shown in Table 1.1).

---

*The concept of "human capital" will be further discussed in Chapter 4.

There are two ways in which women may be discriminated against in
admission to top-ranked universities: (1) there may be explicit or
implicit sex ratios for admission, or (2) more subtly, women may
be denied adequate financial aid that would be available for equally
qualified young men, so that even for those women admitted, enrollment may be impossible, or continuing, difficult.

Inequality in Admission, by Sex

At Harvard, there are 5 men to 2 women;* Yale, which until
recently was an all-male undergraduate institution, now sets its
target as 3:2; Stanford revised its numerical sex ratio policy in 1971
to read: "The ratio of men to women admitted to the University shall
be determined by the nature of the applicant pool with due regard to
specific University strengths."[24]
Public universities have been as reluctant as their private
counterparts to admit equal numbers of women to undergraduate
status. The House hearings on "Discrimination Against Women"
cited the University of North Carolina catalog, which indicated that
"a few exceptional women" would be admitted; the University of Vir-
ginia was reported in the same hearings as having rejected in 1964
"21,000 women but not one man."[25] And, as Cross pointed out, it
is difficult to understand why "a respected state university accepted
83 percent of the men and only 52 percent of the women ranking in
the second tenth of their class."[26] Even those universities that approach equality in numbers of men and women admitted may achieve
a similar discriminatory enrollment by admitting women to undergraduate schools of education and nursing, while preserving male
predominance in the undergraduate arts and science college (from
which aspiration to graduate and professional programs is both more
likely and more possible). Although there has been some modifica-
tion of these policies in recent years, substantial inequality of the
sexes persists in the undergraduate enrollment of many top-ranked
universities and colleges.

Inequality of Financial Aid, by Sex

One important effect of the discriminatory admissions policy
of top-ranked universities is the lesser financial aid available for
women than for men. The reason is twofold: those women admitted
to the prestigious institutions with greater financial resources do not

---

*Harvard's proposed "equal access" policy is discussed in
Chapter 5.

receive an equal share with young men of available scholarship funds; women denied admission to these institutions are diverted to smaller institutions, or to women's colleges, which have fewer funds to distribute.

As previously noted, funds at the disposal of educational institutions are unequally distributed. A major proportion of student financial aid comes directly from the institution; among the institutions, only a handful have the endowment income and reputation that attracts government contracts and foundation grants. Financial aid therefore is concentrated in the relatively few top-ranked universities and colleges that admit fewer undergraduate women. Thus while some bright women are the victims of admission quotas, even successful women applicants may not be offered sufficient funds to permit top-caliber women from low-income families to attend top-flight colleges and universities. For example, while 42 percent of the young men entering the Harvard class of 1974 received financial aid, only 27 percent of the much smaller Radcliffe group were so aided.[27] Young women denied scholarship aid that would be available to an equally qualified young man may lower their sights to a less-prestigious but less-costly school. Both society and young women thus lose out in terms of lifetime career productivity.

The smaller colleges where women are a larger proportion of the student body cannot provide as much financial aid as the larger universities or top liberal arts colleges. In a survey of college sophomores nationwide in 1969-70 Haven and Horch found the average financial aid to men to be $1,000, to women $786. The average institutionally administered grant or scholarship was $671 for men, $515 for women.[28] This channeling of women to less-prestigious colleges and universities is doubly unfortunate because, in addition to providing less financial aid, many of the smaller schools offer less opportunity for continuing on to graduate or professional study.

A further unfortunate consequence of these discriminatory financial aid policies is that women have been forced to seek greater amounts in loans--the average college loan to women was $491, to men $309. And, as a final Catch-22, a corresponding discrimination in the job market means that after graduation women are likely to earn lower salaries (as compared to male graduates) from which the loan repayment must be made.

Supporting institutions, such as the National Merit Scholarship program, likewise favor young men over young women. It is not unusual for several top colleges and universities to compete in scholarship offers for a National Merit Scholar, selected by a qualifying examination taken by boys and girls in the high school junior year. Curiously, over the nearly 20 years of that competitive examination, about twice as many boys as girls have been "discovered"

in the annual "search for talent." (In 1970 approximately 2,000 boys
and 1,000 girls were designated as Merit Scholars, based on examination scores coupled with information on "leadership ability" and
the like.) By contrast, the record of SAT scores over several
decades shows the two sexes with similar composite averages (girls
slightly higher on verbal, boys slightly higher on math portions of
the test). One might be led to ponder the possible bias in the National
Merit exams, or the selection criteria on which National Merit scholars are chosen. The 1970 selection committee of the National Merit
Scholarship Corporation was composed of 13 men, including admissions officers of Stanford, California Institute of Technology, Yale,
Illinois, Cornell, Wisconsin, and Vanderbilt, joined by 3 women,
one a college counselor in a Milwaukee high school, the others admission officers from the University of Chicago and Point Park
College.[29]

Other discriminatory financial aid policies should be noted at
least briefly. The discrimination in school sports programs in public high schools, mentioned earlier in this chapter, contributes to
the almost complete absence of athletic scholarships for young women,
while such scholarships often permit men from lower-income families to attend top-ranked undergraduate institutions.

Federal tax funds likewise support discriminatory policies in
higher education. Direct governmental scholarships, whether in
ROTC or similar programs, or through veteran's benefits, are only
rarely available to women. Federal student aid financed from taxes
(National Direct Student Loan, Work Study, Educational Opportunity
Grants [EOG]) in 1972 (latest available data) was distributed almost
equally with respect to numbers of each sex, but the U.S. Department of Health, Education, and Welfare could provide no breakdown
in terms of dollars awarded by sex;[30] thus any inequality in the
amount of tax-derived funds awarded by sex is masked. Moreover,
since scholarship funds are awarded only to students accepted by a
college or university, and since two to three times as many males as
females are accepted at prestigious high-tuition institutions, taxpayers can be presumed to be spending much more to finance directly
the education of young men.

The federal Basic Educational Opportunity Grant (BEOG) program initiated in 1972 a policy aimed at improving the college opportunities of high school graduates from lower-income families. However, the unusually talented young man from a low-income family,
who has a high SAT or National Merit rating, would in many cases
have been recruited by top schools and provided the necessary funding; the BEOG program will merely shift part of the burden to the
taxpayers as the institution decreases its share of aid to that student.
A young woman of equal ability, with much less chance of a full

scholarship from such an institution, will continue to be restricted to the less prestigious schools for which the BEOG grant (1975 maximum $1,400) is adequate to cover tuition and related costs. (We might note in passing that the BEOG program has never been fully funded, and the amounts awarded until recently have been below the amount projected, affecting both student and institutional awards.)

This sex-discriminatory situation applies also at the state level. Many states have recently begun programs of "equalizing grants," with the explicit and commendable purpose of preserving the diversity of higher education by permitting students to choose a private institution with higher tuition than that charged at state schools. For example, private institutions in New York receive "Bundy" grants, based on the numbers of students to whom they award bachelor's degrees ($800), master's degrees ($600), and doctorates ($3,000).[31] Since women are so poorly represented at Cornell, for example, New York taxpayers are subsidizing the education of young men (not all of whom are New York residents) at the expense of resident young women. To pursue the point a little further, since the median income of parents of entering freshmen at private universities was better than $14,000 in 1969,[32] while the median income of New Yorkers generally was $10,617,[33] the inference may be drawn that the education of relatively affluent young men is apparently being subsidized at the expense of less affluent New Yorkers, especially of less affluent young women, themselves often working and taxpayers, as they attend lower-cost state colleges. Other studies have indicated that it may also be true of state universities, that poorer taxpayers are subsidizing the more costly education (through the doctorate and professional degrees) of children from high-income families attending state universities, since children from lower-income families typically attend low-cost, public four-year, or community colleges.[34]

Finally, although this study is focused on discrimination against women as undergraduates, on the premise that this to a great extent determines the smaller numbers of women in graduate and professional studies, it is worth noting that the 1970 study by Helen Astin indicated that only 46 percent of women doctoral candidates received financial support from the government or their institutions, compared to 58 percent of the men--this despite the Astin evidence that 91 percent of women doctorates were found to be working in their fields a decade after receiving their degrees.[35] In this connection, since education is in our society an accumulation of "certification," the women who were channeled by the admission and financial-aid system to the lesser-known undergraduate institutions tend to experience greater difficulty in winning acceptance for graduate and professional study at the top universities in each field, where chances for institutional and federal grants are greatest. In addition, subsequent possibility of faculty appointments, as well as for jobs in business and government, are greatly affected by the prestige of the graduate institution attended.

Expenditure per student in 1969-70 was highest at private universities ($5,533) and public universities ($3,621) and lowest at public two-year colleges ($941).[36] Such concentration of funds contributes to the excellence of the leading institutions, and to the support of research activity that benefits society; but where enrollments are sex discriminatory, such concentration prevents women from sharing in such excellence as undergraduates. For example:

1. Fifty universities accounted for almost two-thirds of all academic memberships on advisory committees of federal departments in 1974. Such advisory committees and review boards affect the amount of research grants awarded, and thus the research opportunities for women attending other institutions.[37]

2. Institutions in the top 100 recipients of federal research and development support received 85 percent of the nearly $2 billion in U.S. funds allocated for such activities in 1973.[38] "The principal conclusion" of a 1962 study of institution quality was that "institutions with substantial federal financial support had considerably more distinguished faculty members (measured by Guggenheims, membership in scholarly societies) than less well-financed institutions."[39]

3. The "major" institutions provide more opportunity for selection as Woodrow Wilson fellows, and thus women attending lesser institutions have fewer opportunities for financial aid and admission to leading graduate institutions. The "most selective" undergraduate colleges, with less than 10 percent of baccalaureate degrees, produced almost one-fourth of the Wilson Fellows in 1970. Women were less than one-third of the designates.[40]

4. Less than 25 percent of all higher education institutions granting the bachelor's degree produced 75 percent of those who went on to receive the doctorate, in the period 1958-66. Of the top 30 baccalaureate-source institutions, 24 were also found among the top 30 doctorate-granting institutions.[41]

5. With respect generally to admission to graduate school, law, or other top professional schools, graduates of highly ranked undergraduate colleges have better chances. As President Bok was quoted, "most Harvard graduates would be assured of a seat in law school."[42] Similarly, Stanford University reported: "only Harvard, Yale and Princeton have produced more Rhodes Scholars; Stanford students regularly win more Fulbright Scholarships than those of any other institution except U.C. Berkeley; sixteen Stanford faculty members won Guggenheim fellowships in 1973-74," leading the nation in that respect.[43]

6. Major private universities received about 40 percent of the total dollar support from private business and foundations in 1973-74, estimated at about $1 billion.[44] Women were outnumbered by better than 3:2 at these institutions benefiting from tax-exempt gifts.

To sum up, women are being denied equal opportunity with men for admission and financial aid at the institutions that provide the greatest selection of able faculty and research facilities, that control the greatest portion of financial aid, and that offer the best chance for entrance into prestigious and rewarding professional careers. Private universities and other nonprofit organizations are granted tax exemptions on the premise that they are performing a public service by educating the nation's youth; they are not performing that public service when they educate only the male half of the youthful population. Even more forcefully, when these prestigious institutions are the recipients of federal research contracts, or of federal and state scholarship funds, or of private gifts that earn their donors tax exemptions, or the institution benefits by income- or property-tax exemptions, it is the public treasury that is actually providing much of the funds. Taxpayers, men and women, expect their tax monies to be distributed equitably. If this is not the case, such discriminatory institutions must revert to the status of small, private clubs, educating out of their members' pockets a small group outside the mainstream of American life.

Some may question the right or, more accurately, the wisdom of government "intervention" or "control" of higher education. The disappearance of the private sector in higher education would indeed constitute a great loss to the national welfare. Private institutions of higher education have produced most of the Nobel laureates of recent decades. Yet education is "vested with the public interest." The young person seeking higher education in order to improve life-time income is at the same time filling the needs of society. As economist John Hughes pointed out,

> In most cases, the pursuit of private gain will lead
> also to social gain, as for example, a student, at-
> tracted by the high fees of medicine and repelled by
> the low wages of bank clerking, becomes a doctor;
> and, while making eight to ten times the life-time
> earnings of a bank clerk, also provides society
> with services it values eight to ten times more
> highly than those of a bank clerk. . . . A society
> with many doctors will see more of its children
> and adolescents live to become productive adults,
> and such a society will thus recover more of the

costs of the early dependent years than a society
with fewer doctors.[45]

Recent events have proved, moreover, that just as we need an
independent press and judiciary we likewise require for national
welfare an independent source of informed criticism. For this reason society willingly supports private higher education. Yet even
while the state provides funds and tax exemption to private education,
we do collectively regulate such higher education with reference to
the meeting of standards in order to protect the young consumer and
the general public from substandard institutions. College and university degree-granting ceremonies begin with the words, "By the
authority vested in me by the state. . . ." In designating the recipient of tax revenues, state and federal governments have responsibilities to ensure that public funds are not arbitrarily handed over
to the advantage of particular groups in society.

Let us illustrate by an analogy. If the owner of a tennis court
wishes to invite only young men to his private property, and engages
an instructor to teach the fine points of lob and volley, that is his
privilege, and the state cannot order him to admit young women to
the court. If, however, the owner calls on the town and state to roll
the lawns, build enclosures against weather, help pay for the instructors, pay for research on an improved tennis ball, and the like,
the state surely would have an interest in seeing that taxpayers and
their children have equal access to those facilities that their taxes in
large measure provide.

There is indeed, in this period of rising costs, much to be said
for increasing the amount of state and federal aid to private higher
education, to preserve that independent countervailing force. Nevertheless, the granting of any federal or state funds to higher education
requires that the advantages of such education be available equally
to the equally qualified, regardless of sex.

The same is true, of course, for publicly supported higher
education, and for publicly supported vocational education, to which
we now will turn to ask the same question: Are there equal opportunities for young women who wish to develop employable skills in
shop trades or skilled crafts?

Restricted Access to Public Vocational Programs

Across the nation public schools from kindergarten through
high school are now making greater efforts to expose students to a
variety of career options. The federal government has stepped up
funding of vocational education in the high school and postsecondary

years since the passage of the Vocational Education Act of 1963 and its 1968 amendments. It is now generally accepted that high school graduates of both academic and vocational programs need additional training for skilled jobs in business and industry. If we look at the data on vocational training programs funded by federal, state, and local governments, we see once again a sex-stereotyped pattern of enrollment. Fewer young women than young men are being trained for employment in industry and skilled trades--to become carpenters, electricians, mechanics, or welders. Partly this reflects the tracking system from junior high and high school years.

Until Title IX (see Appendix A) was passed in 1972, girls and boys almost everywhere in the United States were assigned either to home arts or to manual arts (shop) courses. In a few school systems girls were permitted to enroll in shop courses, but widespread complaints indicate that traditional sex stereotypes were reinforced by administrative decisions that prevented girls from learning the rudiments of woodworking, metalworking, mechanics, electrical systems, and similar fields. It follows that few young women have recognized their interests and abilities in these fields during their school years. Thus, in vocational training also, the enrollment pattern in part can be attributed to the lesser numbers of girls and young women aspiring to training in skilled crafts. But just as was the case with academic institutions in the years beyond high school, so also postsecondary vocational institutions often refuse to admit those young women who do have the requisite aspiration and capability.

Sometimes the exclusion of young women from postsecondary vocational education is accomplished by administrative decree, listing prerequisite courses in shop or manual arts to which many young girls were denied access in junior high and high school. Or there may be more subtle channeling of young women to one type of program, and young men to other types, as indicated in the 1974 report of the U.S. General Accounting Office:

> Catalogs describing vocational programs used the exclusive pronoun "he" when referring to course requirements in almost all subjects, and the exclusive pronoun "she" when describing secretarial and nursing courses. Vocational officials agreed that potential students studying this material might get the impression that courses were restricted to members of one sex.
> Sometimes classes were physically located in a manner which could encourage sex role stereotyping. In one secondary area vocational school,

> clerical, health, and cosmetology courses were of-
> fered in one building and all other courses in an ad-
> jacent building. Female students questioned by us
> about their vocational interests said the course they
> were taking did not necessarily coincide with what
> they hoped to do later. They said their choices for
> training were limited because girls were not allowed
> in the "boys' building." The school director agreed
> that girls might get that impression but said that
> girls could apply for courses offered in the other
> building. [46]

Both in high school and in postsecondary education, course
offerings to each sex reflect the bias of administrators in state departments of education, high schools, and vocational schools as to
which are "men's jobs" and which "women's." But jobs, with rare
exceptions, are sexless. The Department of Labor reported on the
comparative performance of men and women in 22 aptitude areas;
there was no difference between the sexes in 14 areas, women excelled in 6, and men in 2 (see Table 2.2). In spite of such evidence,
school vocational administrators persist in directing girls to a limited number of traditional "women's" skills and away from shop or
crafts courses.

Willie Mays, interviewed for the television replay of the Giants-
Dodgers playoff in 1951, recalled that he felt inadequate on being
brought up to the major leagues and that he asked Durocher to send
him back to the minors. It is not surprising that even so great an
athlete as the 19-year-old Mays might question his own ability; all
teen-agers share such doubts and need reassurance and support to
develop their potential. Young women teen-agers interested in entering the skilled trades do not get that support and generally do not
develop their potential in these areas.

In the following sections, then, we will find that the options for
women are generally narrower than for men with respect to skill
training for satisfying and well-paid careers. We will look in turn
at postsecondary vocational programs publicly funded, terminal-
occupational programs of higher education, apprentice training, and
federal training programs.

Postsecondary Vocational/Technical Schools (publicly funded)

Since the passage of the Vocational Education amendments of
1963 and 1968 many states have concentrated on regional or area
vocational-technical schools as a replacement for vocational schools

TABLE 2.2

Comparisons of the Performance of Men and Women in Selected Aptitude Areas

Aptitude	Group with higher average performance
U.S. EMPLOYMENT SERVICE	
Numerical reasoning	------------------
Spatial reasoning	Male
Form perception	Female
Clerical perception	Female
Motor coordination	Female
Finger dexterity	Female
Manual dexterity	------------------
HUMAN ENGINEERING LABORATORY	
Abstract visualization	Female
Analytical reasoning	------------------
Eyedness	------------------
Finger dexterity	Female
Foresight	------------------
Grip	Male
Graphoria (accounting aptitude)	Female
Ideaphoria (flow of ideas in verbal pursuits)	Female
Inductive reasoning	------------------
Memory for design	------------------
Number memory	------------------
Observation	Female
Objective personality	------------------
Pitch discrimination	------------------
Rhythm memory	------------------
Silograms (word association)	Female
Structural visualization	Male
Subjective personality	------------------
Timbre discrimination	------------------
Tonal memory	------------------
Tweezer dexterity	------------------
Vocabulary (English)	------------------

NOTE: Dashes indicate no significant difference. Although the differences shown are statistically significant, in most cases they would be of little practical significance. To illustrate, USES research has found spatial reasoning to be important for many of the skilled trades. But the level required exceeds an employed worker average for only one trade. Studies of seniors in high schools throughout the country showed that 67 percent of the boys and 62 percent of the girls equal or exceed this average. This means that more than half the girls have at least the minimum amount of spatial reasoning needed for most skilled trades.

Source: J. N. Hedges and S. E. Bemis, "Sex Stereotyping: Its Decline in Skilled Trades," Monthly Labor Review, U.S. Department of Labor, May 1974, Table 4, p. 19.

linked to city or town high schools. The advantages of the area approach are that the combined resources of several school districts
can provide better equipment and training than a smaller district
can finance on its own. These advantages, however, are less available to young women, who are often left to pursue office practice
studies in aging high schools, or at their own expense in proprietary
schools (private, for profit). As Table 2.3 indicates, women were
only 40 percent of U.S. enrollment in state-approved postsecondary
vocational institutions in 1969; the preliminary report of the Office
for Civil Rights study cited in Chapter 1[47] indicates that women were
still only 40 percent of total January 1974 enrollment in public postsecondary area vocational schools. Of the 227,000 women enrolled
in 1974, over two-thirds were enrolled in business programs and
health fields in these institutions.

Overall, as the NCES study shown in Table 2.4 indicates,
women were only 41 percent of 1973-74 enrollment in public noncollegiate postsecondary schools. Men were 93 percent of enrollment in technical programs and 87 percent in trades and industry
programs; women were 91 percent of health program enrollment and
83 percent in business/office training. However, women were 54
percent of enrollment in private postsecondary vocational training in
the same study.

The discrimination here in tax-supported public facilities is
manifold:

1. Women are actually excluded by administrative decision
from admission to some public postsecondary institutions. New
vocational-technical schools are still being built with inadequate toilet
facilities or lockers for women, and this is subsequently put forth
as a reason for maintaining single-sex schools.

2. More places are provided in publicly funded schools for
training in traditional "men's" fields than in traditional "women's"
occupations. Thus even among those young women who wish to take
office, health, or cosmetology programs, many cannot be admitted
because of "lack of space."

3. By a variety of devices--by catalogs and brochures showing
only male students in trade and industry programs, and women at
typewriters; by labeling of men's and women's programs; by guidance
counseling; by aptitude testing that presumes familiarity based on
high school courses from which girls were excluded--young women
are deterred from enrolling in better-paying trade and industry or
technical fields. Thus these tax-supported vocational schools are
being used to perpetuate sex discrimination in employment and lifetime earnings.

TABLE 2.3

Enrollment in Postsecondary Vocational Education Classes, by Program, by Grade Level, and by Sex, Fiscal Year 1969

Program	Total	Male	Male as Percentage of Total	Female	Female as Percentage of Total	Grade 13	Grade 14
Total	706,085	423,306	60.0	232,779	40.0	491,556	214,529
Agriculture	15,816	14,663	92.7	1,153	7.3	10,618	5,198
Distributive	60,718	45,036	74.2	15,682	25.8	43,181	17,537
Health	91,922	6,886	7.5	85,036	92.5	71,675	20,247
Home economics	13,490	2,123	15.7	11,367	84.3	9,763	3,727
Office	218,448	81,910	37.5	136,538	62.5	151,859	66,589
Technical	130,564	119,834	91.8	10,730	8.2	81,207	49,357
Trades and industry	174,201	152,294	87.4	21,907	12.6	122,562	51,639
Other	926	560	60.5	366	39.5	691	235

Source: U.S. Department of Health, Education, and Welfare, Division of Vocational and Technical Education, Annual Report, Fiscal Year 1969, Table 8.

TABLE 2.4

Women as a Percentage of Enrollment in Noncollegiate
Postsecondary Public Schools with
Occupational Programs
(aggregate U.S. 1973-74)

Type of Program	Women as Percent
Agribusiness	6.7
Marketing and distribution	45.2
Health	91.2
Home economics	84.2
Business/office	83.4
Technical	7.1
Trades and industrial	13.3
Average	41.0

Source: Adapted from U.S. Department of Health, Education,
and Welfare, National Center for Educational Statistics, draft of
preliminary report, 1973-74 enrollment noncollegiate postsecondary
schools with occupational programs (Washington, D.C., March 1976).

Terminal-Occupational Programs
in Higher Education--Two-Year
and Four-Year Institutions

Most of the enrollment in vocational (nondegree) programs in
institutions of higher education (for both men and women) is found
in public two-year systems, such as community colleges (see
Table 1.1). In this fast-growing sector of higher education, administrators have done well in meeting demands for training courses as
new employment areas have opened up in computer and health technology. Nevertheless, these administrators still carry the "freight
of custom" and tend to recruit and encourage women for one set of
occupations and men for another[48] (see Table B.3). Such sex-
stereotyped admissions for courses or schools discriminate against
young women and their tax-paying parents by offering them, for the
same tuition (and tax burden), a lesser set of skills than is provided
for young men. Thus young women are encouraged to enroll in medical technician, secretarial, or key punch programs, while young
men are concentrated in office administration or trade or technical
fields, with easily predictable effects on future advancement opportunities and earnings.

Apprentice Training

     In the hearings on "Discrimination against Women, "Represen-
tative Edith Green several times pointed out that figures on women
in apprenticeship were hard to come by, citing a previous estimate
of 1 percent of total apprenticeships. At this writing such figures
continue to be unavailable in published form. However, a computer
printout furnished by the Bureau of Apprenticeship Training shows
women in 1974 (the latest data) as .9 percent of all registered apprenticeships (see Table B.2). Additional information is provided
by the Equal Employment Opportunity Commission (EEOC). Under
its mandate to ensure that women and minorities are being given
equal access to employment opportunity, the EEOC requires reports
from joint union-management apprenticeship committees having 5
or more apprentices in its entire program (and with employer having
25 or more employees and union having 25 or more members, or
operating a hiring hall).
     Reporting is thus mandatory only for the larger unions, firms,
and apprenticeship programs, which for that reason may be presumed to be more likely to make use of related training programs
involving public school facilities and faculty. Women were only .3
percent of all being trained under these apprenticeship programs in
1972; cosmetology apprenticeships, where women are more numer-
ous, would only rarely be required to file, because of small numbers
involved in union and management.
     Of the 20 states for which the 1972 EEOC data are available,
four had no women apprentices in 1972; Delaware (with only four
women apprentices) had the highest percentage (1.5 percent), while
the New York percentage was .3, California .3, Illinois .2, and so
on. (For data on individual states, see the tables in Chapter 3.)
     An excellent article from the Wisconsin Division of Apprentice-
ship entitled "Women in Apprenticeship--Why Not?" sets forth the
record of that department's effort to secure women apprenticeships
in 1971. The women (who were usually older than the average male
apprentice) proved to be competent, reliable, and respected addi-
tions to the employer's work force.[49] The U.S. Department of
Labor reported in 1970 the variety of fields in which women held
apprenticeships across the United States as pipe fitters, jet engine
assemblers, and other highly skilled trades.[50] These isolated suc-
cesses, however, merely raise more strongly the question of the
grossly unequal distribution of women and men in these skilled fields.
     Unions in skilled trades have been almost exclusively male and
young women have not been encouraged to seek apprenticeship. (In
the Wisconsin study, one mill listed apprenticeship opportunities in
the men's washroom.)[51] This is not to say that large numbers of

young women have been rejected for such apprenticeship (no data are available). A combination of factors may discourage women from applying: lack of female role-models in such fields; the lack of "connections" within the informal network in which information about apprenticeships is provided (even more true for minority young men); the denial of shop courses in public schools, reinforced by the lack of access to vocational and trades training in postsecondary schools.

An excellent study of the occupational education program in the Boston public schools reported the comment of the associate superintendent for curriculum and instruction as to why girls were not given training for more lucrative fields: "The union might object." In the same system, the director of the Department of Vocational Education and Industrial Arts and the associate superintendent for guidance also objected to training girls for trades with strong "male" unions.[52]

Training under Federal Manpower
Development and Training Act
(since 1976, Employment and
Training Act [ETA])

Women were only 34 percent of those being trained under the institutional training program of the Manpower Development and Training Act (MDTA) and 22 percent of those in on-the-job training in fiscal year 1974 (see Table 1.1). An explanation for the lower percentage of women in such federally funded training is found in the Wisconsin study cited above, describing the referral procedure by which applicants to the State Employment Service are directed to training opportunities.

> It has been customary for Employment Service counselors to keep listed job openings in separate file boxes on each desk so that a woman applicant without professional qualifications, or for whom there is no appropriate professional job opening, will be asked if she can type. If she can, she is shunted to "clerical"; if not, she is offered (from another box) a range of unskilled jobs in retailing, medical facility, hotel or institutional work. Such entry-level jobs as food service worker, waitress, or aide not only pay rock bottom wages but are dead end. The Bureau of Apprenticeship and Training has excluded all occupations in the clerical and retail areas from its list of trades that may be considered for formal apprenticeship approval.[53]

It is understandable that the often overworked employment in-
terviewers of a state employment service do not have unlimited time
in which to explore the possibilities of each job seeker. The market
for clerical workers is usually good, at least in comparison to more
specific occupational fields. Since women are assumed "naturally"
to be born possessing the desired qualities for clerical work, it
seems to satisfy both the goals of the employment service (more
placements) and of the applicant (a job) immediately thus to classify
all women. Since a man is likewise assumed "naturally" to lack
these clerical skills it is necessary to train him for some field. If
he shows the necessary aptitude, depending on funding and programs
available, he can then enter a variety of MDTA (ETA) programs that
may lead to skill development in mechanical, electrical, automotive,
or other areas.

As in the union/management-sponsored apprentice training
programs, public high school or postsecondary facilities may be used
in such instruction. Once more, young women and their tax-paying
parents are short-changed, since whatever training (if any) a woman
receives is likely to be short term. Usually such training leads to
employment in low-skilled clerical or health-care fields. Institutional training, using school facilities and faculty time, is expensive.
Likewise, the on-the-job training, JOBS-Optional, or other programs
oriented toward male unemployed and underemployed use tax-derived
funds for wage subsidies or related expenditures.

The use of public funds for training and upgrading of men,
rather than women, represents another example of women's restricted educational opportunities. Taxpayers who fund those programs are entitled to an equal chance for their children, boys or
girls, young men or young women, to develop skills that will lead to
a well-paid and satisfying career.

SUMMARY

The distribution of both academic and vocational education resources in the United States has been shown in this chapter to be
weighted toward giving many young men the skills leading toward
satisfying and well-paid lifetime careers; for young women, the emphasis has been on providing fewer young women with skills requiring
a relatively short training period that will fit them for not-very-well-
paid jobs during a working life, which is incorrectly assumed to be a
brief interlude between high school graduation and marriage.

Such an education and training policy is based on a concept of
women's employment patterns that does not fit the observed facts.
The majority of women in the labor force are married, often supporting

themselves and other dependents as well; the average working woman
will spend 20 or 30 years in the labor force. Thus academic and
vocational education should provide women with skills fitting them
for careers, rather than for temporary employment.

Although postsecondary education is subsidized by the federal
government, policies are determined at the state and institutional
level; thus it is essential to examine the distribution of the sexes in
education within each state. Therefore for each of 20 states--
Arkansas, California, Colorado, Delaware, Florida, Illinois, Kansas,
Massachusetts, Michigan, Mississippi, Nevada, New Jersey, New
York, Ohio, Oklahoma, Pennsylvania, South Carolina, Texas, Vermont, Wyoming--in Chapter 3 we will look at the distribution of enrollment in academic and vocational education and the extent to which
taxpayers, parents of girls as well as boys, are supporting a postsecondary education system that denies young women equal opportunity for interesting and rewarding careers.

NOTES

1. Harvard University and Radcliffe College, Report of the
Committee to Consider Aspects of the Harvard-Radcliffe Relationship that Affect Administrative Arrangements, Admissions, Financial Aid, and Educational Policy, Cambridge, Mass., February 26,
1975.

2. Women on Words and Images, Dick and Jane as Victims
(Princeton, N.J.: Women on Words and Images, 1972), pp. 64-68.

3. U.S. Department of Health, Education, and Welfare,
Trends in Post-secondary Education (Washington, D.C., 1970),
p. 188.

4. Philip Goldberg, in TransAction, April 1968, pp. 28-30.

5. U.S. Department of Health, Education, and Welfare, op.
cit., p. 5.

6. Patricia Cross, Beyond the Open Door (San Francisco:
Jossey-Bass, 1971), Table 1, p. 20.

7. Joanne Coakley, "Attitudes of Guidance Counsellors," in
Report of the Massachusetts Governor's Commission on the Status
of Women, Appendix E (Boston, 1972).

8. U.S. Congress, House, Hearings before the Subcommittee
on Equal Opportunities of the Committee on Education and Labor,
93rd Cong., 1st sess., H.R. 208, Part I, p. 189.

9. Coakley, op. cit.

10. College Entrance Examination Board, College-Bound Seniors, 1973-74 (Evanston, Ill.: CEEB, 1974), Table 3, p. 18.

11. U.S. Congress, House, op. cit.; Lucy Sells, "A Pilot Test of Sex in High School Mathematics Preparation," Appendix C (quoted in testimony of Jennifer Ryan, National Student Lobby).

12. J. Flanagan and Associates, The American High School Student (Pittsburgh: University of Pittsburgh, Project Talent, 1964), pp. 5-12.

13. Report of the Massachusetts Governor's Commission on the Status of Women, op. cit., p. 72; U.S. Congress, House, op. cit., pp. 15-25; 187; 433-36.

14. "Careers are Chief Concern of Youth," Richmond News Leader, January 22, 1974, p. 14.

15. College Entrance Examination Board, op. cit., Tables 9 and 10, p. 22.

16. Alice deRivera, "On De-segregating Stuyvesant High," in Sisterhood is Powerful, ed. Robin Morgan (New York: Vintage Books, 1970), pp. 366-75.

17. New regulations have been issued by the Department of Health, Education, and Welfare "to protect vocational students from being cheated and reduce multimillion dollar defaults on federally insured loans. Under the new rules, vocational-technical schools will be required to tell prospective students of how successful graduates were in finding a job. . . . The schools and colleges which prepare students for occupations or careers must also establish refund policies." Boston Globe, February 22, 1975. See also Boston Globe, Spotlight Series, March 31 to May 31, 1974.

18. U.S. Department of Commerce, Bureau of the Census, Educational Attainment, March 1972, Series P-20, No. 243, November 1972, Table E, p. 7.

19. U.S. Department of Commerce, Bureau of the Census, PC-1-634, 1970, Table 200.

20. U.S. Department of Health, Education, and Welfare, Trends in Post-Secondary Education (Washington, D.C., 1970), pp. 188-89.

21. M. Curti and R. Nash, Philanthropy in the Shaping of American Higher Education (New Brunswick, N.J.: Rutgers University Press, 1965), Chapter X.

22. Ibid., p. 222.

23. L. C. Solmon and P. J. Taubman, eds., Does College Matter? (New York: Academic Press, 1973), p. 3.

24. Stanford University, Stanford Observor, March 3, 1973.

25. U.S. Congress, House, Hearings before Special Subcommittee on Education of the Committee on Education and Labor, 91st Cong., 2d sess., Sec. 805 of H.R. 16098, Parts 1 and 2, "Discrimination Against Women."

26. Cross, op. cit., p. 151.

27. Derek Bok, in Harvard Today, Fall 1974, p. 10.

28. E. W. Haven and D. H. Horch, How College Students Finance Their Education (Evanston, Ill.: College Entrance Examination Board, 1972) (quoted in Ruth Ekstrom, Barriers to Women's Participation in Post-Secondary Education: A Review of the Literature [Princeton, N.J.: Educational Testing Service, forthcoming], p. 12).

29. National Merit Scholarship Corporation, Annual Report, 1970 (Evanston, Ill., 1970), Table 7, p. 28 (see Appendix D).

30. See Appendix E, letter from the Department of Health, Education, and Welfare, January 21, 1976.

31. Patricia Walsh, "An Analysis of the Participation by Female Students in the Benefits of the Bundy Program," unpublished study, Boston University, Department of Economics, June 1975. (See N.Y. Sec. 6401 of Education Law [1968] as amended 1973.)

32. American Council on Education, National Norms for Entering College Freshmen, Fall 1969 (Washington, D.C.: ACE, 1970), p. 39 (median interpolated).

33. U.S. Department of Commerce, Bureau of the Census, Characteristics of Population (1970), Table 57, Income in 1969, pp. 34-311.

34. L. Hansen and B. Weisbrod, "Distribution of Costs and Direct Benefits of Public Higher Education: The Case of California," in The Daily Economist, ed. S. H. Johnson and B. Weisbrod (Englewood Cliffs, N.J.: Prentice-Hall, 1973), pp. 132-45.

35. Helen S. Astin, The Woman Doctorate in America (New York: Russell Sage Foundation, 1969).

36. U.S. Department of Health, Education, and Welfare, Financial Statistics of Institutions of Higher Education, 1969-70: Current Funds, Revenues, and Expenditures (Washington, D.C., 1972), pp. 5-6.

37. Murray Weidenbaum, quoted in Boston Globe, August 4, 1974, p. A-91.

38. National Science Foundation, Federal Support to Universities, Colleges and Selected Nonprofit Institutions, FY 1973 (NSF 75-304), Table B-11.

39. H. Orlans, The Effects of Federal Programs on Higher Education, in S. Harris, A Statistical Portrait of Higher Education (New York: McGraw-Hill, 1972), p. 399.

40. Woodrow Wilson Foundation, Annual Report 1970 (Princeton, N.J., 1971), Tables 4, 5, pp. 17-18.

41. National Academy of Sciences, Doctorate Recipients from U.S. Universities, 1956-66 (Washington, D.C., 1967), p. 19.

42. Derek Bok, in Boston Globe, November 11, 1973, p. A-43.

43. R. Anderson, "What Makes a University Great?" (Palo Alto, Calif.: Stanford University, 1974).

44. Council for Financial Aid to Education, Survey of Voluntary Support of Education 1973-74 (New York, 1975).

45. John Hughes, "Who Should Pay for College Education?" Boston University Business Review, Winter 1958.

46. U.S. General Accounting Office, "What Is the Role of Federal Assistance in Vocational Education?" Washington, D.C., December 31, 1974.

47. U.S. Office for Civil Rights, Preliminary Report of January 1974 Enrollment in Public Postsecondary Area Vocational Schools, U.S. Department of Health, Education, and Welfare draft bulletin, March 1976.

48. Report of the Massachusetts Governor's Commission on the Status of Women, op. cit., Tables II, IIA, p. 107.

49. U.S. Department of Labor, Patricia Mapp, Women in Apprenticeship--Why Not? Manpower Research Monograph No. 33 (Washington, D.C., 1974), pp. 23-26.

50. U.S. Department of Labor, Bureau of Apprentice Training, Women in Apprenticeship (Washington, D.C., August 1970), pp. 1-6.

51. U.S. Department of Labor, Mapp, op. cit., p. 13.

52. Gail Bryan, Discrimination on the Basis of Sex in Occupational Education in the Boston Public Schools (Boston: Mayor's Commission on the Status of Women, 1972), pp. 29-31.

53. U.S. Department of Labor, Mapp, op. cit., pp. 15-16.

CHAPTER

3

STATE-BY-STATE ANALYSIS
OF OPPORTUNITIES FOR WOMEN
IN TAX-SUPPORTED
POSTSECONDARY EDUCATION

This chapter sets forth data indicating the sex-discriminatory enrollment pattern of education beyond high school in each of 20 states and the extent to which this pattern is supported by tax-derived funds. There is no question as to the desirability of public support of institutions of higher education, both public and private. In this century technological and scientific advances, as well as improved understanding of the human condition, are to a large extent the product of academic research. If we accept the need for American society to devote a portion of its resources to education beyond high school, in the interest of society as well as of the individual, we must use these resources equitably--that is, no qualified individual should be excluded from access to such tax-supported education. Low-income blacks, Chicanos, and other minorities have rightly protested that their youth do not share equally in opportunities for higher education. Yet the sex discrimination described in Chapter 2, and subsequently in this chapter, poses the question more sharply. In the case of young women, there can be no resort to interminable and unresolvable arguments about the effects of inferior schools, inadequate nutrition, less-supportive family and social environments that might have handicapped them in "qualifying" for education beyond high school.

The high school girl of whatever race, ethnic background, or color has run side by side with her brother through the school years, surmounting the same academic hurdles. All objective evidence attests to their equal competence. Thus if equal numbers of each sex apply for further education, they should be equally represented in each type of institution. This is not the case, as was shown in Table 1.1 and will be shown in tables for each of the states studied in this chapter. Women are a minority in the research universities, outnumbered by about 3:2 in those universities that receive the major portion of state and federal tax funds. Although such concentration of funds is desirable for effective teaching and research, which benefits all taxpayers, the sex-discriminatory enrollment means that fewer young women than young men have the opportunity to engage in such research, to learn from top faculty, to have access to the best library and laboratory facilities, to be encouraged to graduate study, to aspire to become professors, doctors, or lawyers. Women are equally a minority in the public two-year institutions that offer access to youth from lower-income families.

In vocational training, data are less satisfactory, because the U.S. Department of Education since 1969 has ceased to collect enrollment by sex within postsecondary programs for its annual report from all states. In 1969 women were 40 percent of total postsecondary vocational enrollment, with a very low percent in trade and industry or technical programs, and a very high percent in health and office fields. More recent data from subareas of postsecondary vocational training indicate that this distribution persists (see Table 2.4). In vocational programs of public two-year colleges and in federally subsidized apprenticeship and manpower training programs, public tax-supported facilities are likewise used for the benefit of young men rather than young women. In the on-the-job training program, with the best chance for jobs after training, women in 1974 nationally were 22 percent of those enrolled. This bias, not only in the numbers trained, but in the fields of training, results in economic disadvantage for women over a working lifetime.

In this chapter we will look at each state in turn, finding in almost every case a similar pattern of discriminatory enrollment. Then in Chapter 4 we will seek to explain the motivation of the leaders of American education who have established and perpetuated this pattern.

The 20 states covered here include almost two-thirds of the total U.S. population and are thus representative of the U.S. education beyond high school for a majority of our youth. The omission of the other 30 states was intended only to economize on research time. It does not imply that there are no "national" universities, top-level liberal arts colleges, or extensive systems of two-year colleges and vocational institutions in these states. Neither should the omission be taken to indicate that the education system of the omitted states is any less sex discriminatory than those 20 whose record is included here: Arkansas, California, Colorado, Delaware, Florida, Illinois, Kansas, Massachusetts, Michigan, Mississippi,

Nevada, New Jersey, New York, Ohio, Oklahoma, Pennsylvania, South Carolina, Texas, Vermont, and Wyoming.*

ARKANSAS

The Governor's Commission on the Status of Women released in 1972 a study of career aspirations of young women in Arkansas.† The young women responding expressed realistic attitudes about their future life roles; more than three-fourths disagreed with the statement, "Most girls will become housewives and never work outside the home." An overwhelming 96 percent believed that "a woman should be able to hold and be promoted in whatever job for which she prepares herself." Yet young women in Arkansas, as in other states, seemed unaware that the young woman "is prepared" by the education system and does not have equal opportunity "to prepare herself."

Enrollment

As Table 3.1 indicates, girls in 1973 were just about half the high school graduates, yet were only 44 percent of the full-time degree-credit undergraduate enrollment in the state, and only 41 percent at the top-ranking University of Arkansas. At the public two-year colleges women were only 36 percent of enrollment in degree programs. Of the 3,217 bachelor's degrees received by Arkansas women in 1972, 51 percent were in education.

---

*Basic data regarding these states are reflected in Tables 3.1 through 3.20, derived from the sources listed after Table 3.1. Additional background data on individual states, which is discussed in the text, comes from the following: Education Commission of the States, Higher Education in the States 5, no. 1 (Denver, Col., 1975); U.S. Department of Health, Education, and Welfare, Residence and Migration of College Students, Fall 1968 (Washington, D.C., 1970) (latest data by sex); U.S. Department of Health, Education, and Welfare, National Center for Educational Statistics, Earned Degrees Conferred, 1971-72 (Washington, D.C., 1972), Tables 1, 3A, 3B, 8, 9, pp. 180-93; and Warren Willingham, Free Access: Higher Education (New York: College Entrance Examination Board, 1970).

†Governor's Commission on the Status of Women--Task Force on Education and Counseling, Education and Counseling Status Report of Young Men and Women: A Survey of Senior Students from Fourteen Public Secondary Schools in Arkansas (Little Rock, December, 1972).

Women were 45 percent of enrollment in nondegree-credit programs in Arkansas higher education. Of the 332 Arkansas apprenticeships reported in 1972, none were women, Under the federally funded manpower training programs, women in Arkansas were 37 percent of those in institutional training.

Funding from Taxes

More than 50 percent of the fiscal year 1973 state tax funds appropriated for higher education went to the University of Arkansas and the associated Medical Center; over 60 percent of federal obligations to Arkansas higher education went to these same institutions. Arkansas women in 1972 received 15 percent of doctorates granted by state institutions and among first-professional degrees 8 percent of the degrees in medicine, and 3 percent in law.

The $4.6 million of federal, state, and local funds expended in fiscal year 1974 for postsecondary vocational education appears to have been used to train about three young men for every two young women, if Arkansas follows the national trend (see Table 2.4). We can assume that expenditure of tax-derived funds in public two-year colleges reflects the somewhat higher percent of young men in these programs. Likewise, federal and state funds used for major apprenticeship programs in Arkansas benefit young men only. The almost $4 million of federal funds obligated under institutional and on-the-job training benefit more than three young men for every two young women.

CALIFORNIA

California has long been a national leader in providing education beyond high school for its citizens, in both academic and vocational areas. State tax funds appropriated for higher education in 1972-73 were over $850 million. Yet although women in 1973 were slightly better than half the high school graduates, they have not been represented in equal numbers with men in postsecondary education.

Enrollment

Women in 1973 were only 41 percent of the full-time degree-credit undergraduate enrollment in California institutions, representing almost 90,000 fewer women than men at this level. In

TABLE 3.1

Opportunities for Women in Education Beyond High School in Arkansas

| | Enrollment in Postsecondary Institutions | | | Financial Support (in millions of dollars) | | | |
| | | | | Tax-Exempt Funds, 1973-74[1] | | Tax Funds Fiscal Year 1973 | |
	Women	Total	Women as Percent of Total	Private Business	Private Foundations	State Tax Funds[2]	Federal Obligations[3]
1973 high school graduates[4]	12,796	25,705	50				
I. Academic (degree credit) enrollment							
Fall 1973 full-time undergraduate enrollment, public and private (nonprofit), state total	17,181	39,090	44	n.a.	n.a.	56.4	21.1
A. Research universities*[5]							
Public (University of Arkansas--main campus)	3,405	8,313	41	n.a.	.2	21.2[a]	8.8[b]
Private	--	--	--	--	--	--	--
B. Excluding research universities							
Public, total	10,140	22,903	44	n.a.	n.a.	n.a.	n.a.
Universities	3,139	7,071	44	n.a.	n.a.	n.a.	n.a.
Other four-year	6,658	14,875	45	n.a.	n.a.	n.a.	n.a.
Two-year	343	957	36	n.a.	n.a.	2.4	n.a.
Private, total	3,636	7,874	46	n.a.	n.a.	n.a.	n.a.
Universities	--	--	--	--	--	--	--
Other four-year	3,341	7,192	46	n.a.	n.a.	n.a.	n.a.
Two-year	295	682	43	n.a.	n.a.	n.a.	n.a.

Expenditures, Fiscal Year 1974[8]

	State/Local	Federal
	3.8	.8

	Women	Total	Women as Percent of Total
II. Vocational enrollment			
A. Fiscal year 1974 enrollment in state-approved postsecondary, total (unduplicated)[6]	n.a.	7,475	40+[7]
Occupations			
Trade and industry		3,141	13
Technical		341	8
Home economics (gainful)		27	84
Health		2,271	92
Office		1,645	62
Distributive		0	26
Other		50	n.a.

B. Fall 1973 full- and part-time enrollment, public and private (nonprofit; nondegree credit) 782 1,754 45

C. Calendar year 1972 apprenticeships, total numbers9 0 332 0

Federal Obligations, Fiscal Year 1974[11] 3.0 .9

D. Fiscal year 1974 MDTA training[10]
Institutional 1,500 37
JOBS Optional/On-the-Job Training n.a. 22‡

n.a. = not available.

aAdditional appropriation: medical center $7.3 million.   bAdditional obligation: medical center $4.0 million.

Notes for Tables 3.1-3.20

*Research universities are defined by the Carnegie Commission on Higher Education as those institutions among the 100 leading institutions in federal financial support over a period of years who awarded at least 50 Ph.D.s (or M.D.s) in 1969-70. See the commission's A Classification of Institutions of Higher Education (Berkeley, Calif.: Carnegie Commission, 1973), pp. 2-3.

†No individual state breakdown by sex. National postsecondary breakdown by sex, fiscal year 1969.

‡No individual state breakdown by sex. National JOBS Optional/On-the-Job Training by sex, fiscal year 1974.

Note: Percentages computed by the author.

Sources:

1. Council for Financial Aid to Education, Survey of Voluntary Support of Education (New York, 1975), pp. 5-6.

2. Council for Financial Aid to Education, Handbook of Aid to Higher Education (New York, 1972), Tables D-1 to D-50, narrative, notes.

3. National Science Foundation, Federal Support to Universities, Colleges, and Selected Non-Profit Institutions, Fiscal Year 1973 (Washington, D.C., 1975), pp. 41, 78-109.

4. U.S. Department of Health, Education, and Welfare, Statistics of Elementary and Secondary Day Schools, Fall 1973 (Washington, D.C., March 1971), Table 8, p. 25.

5. U.S. Department of Health, Education, and Welfare, Fall Enrollment in Higher Education, 1973 (Washington, D.C., 1975), Tables 2, 3, 4, 10 (A-N), 13 (A-N), 20.

6. U.S. Department of Health, Education, and Welfare, Vocational and Technical Education, Fiscal Year 1974 (Washington, D.C., 1974); and idem, Vocational Education Information III (Washington, D.C., 1974), Tables 042-050.

7. U.S. Department of Health, Education, and Welfare, Vocational and Technical Education, Fiscal Year 1969 (Washington, D.C., 1969). (This is the latest annual report with breakdown by sex and program.)

8. U.S. Department of Health, Education, and Welfare, Vocational and Technical Education, Fiscal Year 1974; and idem, Vocational Education Information III, Table 008.

9. Unpublished data from Technical Information Division, Office of Research, Equal Employment Opportunity Commission, Washington, D.C., 1973.

10. U.S. Department of Labor, Manpower Report of the President, 1975 (Washington, D.C., 1975), Tables F-2, F-4, F-9.

11. Ibid., Table F-2.

63

TABLE 3.2

Opportunities for Women in Education Beyond High School in California

	Enrollment in Postsecondary Institutions			Financial Support (in millions of dollars)			
				Tax-Exempt Funds, 1973-74[1]		Tax Funds	
						State Tax Funds, Fiscal Year 1972[2]	Federal Obligations, Fiscal Year 1973[3]
	Women	Total	Women as Percent of Total	Private Business	Private Foundations		
1973 high school graduates[4]	135,682	268,021	51				
I. Academic (degree credit) enrollment							
Fall 1973 full-time undergraduate enrollment, public and private (nonprofit), state total	216,654	522,356	41	n.a.	30.0	853.6	429.1
A. Research universities,*[5] total	30,117	71,174	42	12.9	30.0	224.7[a]	304.2[b]
Public: University of California at							
Berkeley	7,774	19,270	40	1.0	3.9	73.6	58.4
Davis	5,142	11,074	46	.6	1.5	47.4	20.3
Los Angeles	8,773	19,031	46	1.1	2.7	76.4	60.9
San Diego	2,510	5,909	42	.5	1.0	27.3	55.2
Private: California Institute of Technology	101	835	12	2.2	3.2	n.a.	20.4
Stanford University	2,523	6,469	39	5.0	12.6	n.a.	56.9
University of Southern California	3,294	8,586	38	2.5	5.1	n.a.	32.1
B. Excluding research universities							
Public, total	162,355	397,668	41	n.a.	n.a.	n.a.	n.a.
Universities	12,057	25,052	48	n.a.	n.a.	n.a.	n.a.
Other four-year	69,008	163,314	42	n.a.	n.a.	n.a.	n.a.
Two-year	81,290	209,302	39	n.a.	n.a.	175.0	n.a.
Private, total	24,182	53,514	45	n.a.	n.a.	n.a.	n.a.
Universities	2,523	5,378	47	n.a.	n.a.	n.a.	n.a.
Other four-year	21,365	47,465	45	n.a.	n.a.	n.a.	n.a.
Two-year	294	671	44	n.a.	n.a.	n.a.	n.a.

	Expenditures, fiscal year 1974[8]	
	State/Local	Federal
	105.1	--

II. Vocational enrollment			
A. Fiscal year 1974 enrollment in state-approved postsecondary, total (unduplicated)[6]	n.a.	398,911	40[7]
Occupations:			
Trade and industry		105,798	13
Technical		46,666	8
Home economics (gainful)		19,029	84
Health		33,749	92
Office		117,711	62
Distributive		44,100	26
Other		31,858	n.a.
B. Fall 1973 full- and part-time enrollment, public and private (nonprofit; nondegree credit)	144,126	311,831	46
C. Calendar year 1972 apprenticeships, total numbers[9]	76	26,385	.3

			Federal Obligations, Fiscal Year 1974[11]
D. Fiscal year 1974 MDTA training[10]			
Institutional		10,500	26	33.0
JOBS Optional/On-the-Job Training		n.a.	22‡	10.7

[a] Additional appropriations: Hastings College of Law, $1.2 million.

[b] San Francisco Medical Center, $30.9 million.

65

public two-year colleges and in prestigious "research universities, " both public and private, women are outnumbered by about 3:2.

Women were 46 percent of enrollment in nondegree-credit programs in California higher education. Of the 26,000 apprentice-ships reported to the Equal Employment Opportunity Commission in 1972, 76, or .3 percent were women. Under the federally funded manpower training programs, women in California were just about one-fourth of those in institutional training.

Funding from Taxes

About 30 percent of the fiscal year 1972 state tax funds appro-priated for higher education went to the "research universities" where women are outnumbered by almost a 3:2 ratio; about 70 per-cent of fiscal year 1973 federal obligations went to these same in-stitutions. Women in 1972 received 15 percent of all doctorates awarded in California and, among first-professional degrees, 11 per-cent of the degrees in medicine and 8 percent in law.

In addition to appropriations for operating expenses of institu-tions of public higher education, state scholarship funds amounting to more than $32 million were awarded California residents for use in the state in 1974-75; almost 80 percent of the awards went to students attending private colleges and institutions. Since men out-number women in the private sector, the presumption would be that these scholarship dollars would also be biased toward male recipients.

Although we are concerned here with undergraduates, the state Graduate Fellowship program, funded at $1 million in 1974-75, like-wise may safely be assumed to reflect sex-discriminatory distribu-tion, since there were three male graduate students for every two females in 1973. Contracts with private medical schools, funded at just under $2 million in 1974-75, are contingent upon enrollment increases. Since 89 percent of the recipients of degrees in medicine in 1972 were men, as noted above, once more the discriminatory ad-missions patterns ensure that tax-derived funds will be used to train many more young men than young women for this arduous but reward-ing profession.

In addition, 1973-74 business gifts of $13 million and founda-tion grants of $30 million earned their donors tax reductions while contributing toward strengthened faculty, facilities, and research activities of the "research universities." All taxpayers thus involun-tarily subsidized the education of three young men for every two young women, since the taxes not paid by the donors must be made up by the rest of the taxpayers.

The $105 million of state and local funds expended in fiscal year 1974 for postsecondary vocational education likewise appears to have been used to train more young men than young women, if California follows the national trend (see Table 2.4). We can assume that expenditure of tax-derived funds in public two-year colleges reflects the somewhat higher percent of young men in these programs. Likewise, federal and state funds used for major apprenticeship programs in California benefit young men almost exclusively. The $43 million of federal funds obligated in fiscal year 1974 under institutional and on-the-job training programs benefited about three times as many men as women.

COLORADO

Enrollment

The proportion of high school graduates who go on to college has tended to be higher in Colorado than in most states. Girls were a little better than half the high school graduates in the state in 1973, yet they represented only 44 percent of the full-time degree-credit undergraduate enrollment in the state and only 43 percent at the research universities. They were least represented at the University of Colorado (41 percent) and at the public two-year colleges (38 percent).

Women were outnumbered 3:2 in nondegree-credit programs in Colorado higher education in 1973. Of the 2,400 apprenticeships reported in 1972 to the Equal Employment Opportunity Commission, 4, or .2 percent were women. Under the federally funded manpower training programs, women in Colorado were just over one-third of those in institutional training.

Funding from Taxes

About 33 percent of the fiscal year 1973 state tax funds appropriated for higher education went to the research universities and associated medical center; about 75 percent of fiscal year 1973 federal obligations went to these same institutions. Women in 1972 received 15 percent of all doctorates awarded in Colorado, and, among first-professional degrees, 9 percent of the degrees in medicine and 6 percent in law. Women tended to be concentrated in education; of the nearly 6,000 bachelor's degrees received by women in 1972, about one-third were in this field.

TABLE 3.3

Opportunities for Women in Education Beyond High School in Colorado

	Enrollment in Postsecondary Institutions			Financial Support (in millions of dollars)			
			Women as	Tax-Exempt Funds, 1973-74[1]		Tax Funds Fiscal Year 1973	
	Women	Total	Percent of Total	Private Business	Private Foundations	State Tax Funds[2]	Federal Obligations[3]
1973 high school graduates[4]	16,915	33,358	51				
I. Academic (degree credit) enrollment Fall 1973 full-time undergraduate enrollment, public and private (nonprofit), state total	32,097	73,550	44			115.2	64.2
A. Research universities,*[5] total	12,563	29,341	43	n.a.	n.a.	26.6	48.8
Public: University of Colorado (main campus)	6,561	16,054	41	n.a.	n.a.	14.1[a]	32.5
Colorado State University	6,002	13,287	45	.3	.1	12.5	16.3
Private	---	---	--	--	--	--	--
B. Excluding research universities							
Public, total	27,705	64,044	43	n.a.	n.a.	n.a.	n.a.
Universities	1,726	3,734	46	n.a.	n.a.	n.a.	n.a.
Other four-year	11,031	24,769	44	n.a.	n.a.	n.a.	n.a.
Two-year	2,385	6,200	38	n.a.	n.a.	24.6	n.a.
Private, total	4,392	9,506	46	n.a.	n.a.	n.a.	n.a.
Universities	2,044	5,033	41	n.a.	n.a.	n.a.	n.a.
Other four-year	2,348	4,473	52	n.a.	n.a.	n.a.	n.a.
Two-year	---	---	--	--	--	--	--

Expenditures, fiscal year 1974[8]

	State/Local	Federal
	10.7	2.3

II. Vocational enrollment

A. Fiscal year 1974 enrollment in state-approved postsecondary, total (unduplicated)[6] n.a. 19,749 40[+7]

Occupations:

Trade and industry	4,838	13
Technical	4,884	8
Home economics (gainful)	939	84
Health	2,342	92
Office	5,313	62
Distributive	859	26
Other	574	n.a.

B. Fall 1973 full- and part-time enrollment, public and private (nonprofit; nondegree credit) 5,628 13,998 40

C. Calendar year 1972 apprenticeships, total numbers[9] 4 2,421 .2

Federal Obligations, Fiscal Year 1974[11]

D. Fiscal year 1974 MDTA training[10]

Institutional	1,500	36	3.6
JOBS Optional/On-the-Job Training	n.a.	22[‡]	.8

[a] Additional appropriation: $11.7 million for medical center.

The $13 million of federal, state, and local funds expended in fiscal year 1974 for postsecondary vocational education likewise was used to train about three young men for every two young women, if Colorado follows the national trend (see Table 2.4). We can assume that the expenditure of tax-derived funds in public two-year colleges reflects the 3:2 ratio of men to women in these Colorado institutions. Likewise, federal and state funds used for major apprenticeship programs in Colorado benefit young men almost exclusively. The $4.4 million of federal funds obligated in fiscal year 1974 for institutional and on-the-job training were heavily weighted toward the training of men.

DELAWARE

Enrollment

Among Delaware high school graduates in 1973, girls were 52 percent. Young women in Delaware were also closer to equality in undergraduate enrollment in 1973 (47 percent) than in most of the 20 states studied here. However, migration to institutions outside the state is high among Delaware youth; in fall 1968 (the latest published migration study by sex) of the 6,679 Delaware men and 5,030 women who were enrolled in undergraduate higher education, about 3,000 men and 2,000 women were enrolled outside the home state. All candidates for professional degrees (law, medicine, etc.) must go out of state. Thus the more favorable ratio of women to men in within-state enrollment exaggerates the overall ratio of women to men in undergraduate status. Women were only 38 percent of enrollment in degree-credit programs of public two-year colleges.

Delaware is one of three states (the others are Arkansas and Vermont) where women represented a majority of 1973 enrollment in nondegree-credit programs, possibly reflecting the growth of "new careers" training programs oriented toward women's fields. (Since young men are only about one-third of all Delaware enrollments in these nondegree-credit programs, their needs for training are not being fairly met.) However, of the 253 apprenticeships reported to the Equal Employment Opportunity Commission for 1972 women were only 2 percent. Similarly, under the federally funded manpower training programs, women in Delaware were only 36 percent of those in institutional training.

Funding from Taxes

Taxpayers in Delaware are to a slight degree favoring young men over young women in home-state education at the undergraduate

TABLE 3.4

Opportunities for Women in Education Beyond High School in Delaware

	Enrollment in Postsecondary Institutions			Financial Support (in millions of dollars)			
				Tax-Exempt Funds, 1973–74[1]		Tax Funds	
	Women	Total	Women as Percent of Total	Private Business	Private Foundations	State Tax Funds, Fiscal Year 1972[2]	Federal Obligations, Fiscal Year 1973[3]
1973 high school graduates[4]	4,003	7,733	52				
I. Academic (degree credit) enrollment							
Fall 1973 full-time undergraduate enrollment, public and private (nonprofit), state total	7,294	15,362	47	n.a.	n.a.		
Public, total	6,329	13,229	47	n.a.	n.a.	23.1	6.9
Universities	5,249	10,662	49	.2	2.1	n.a.	n.a.
Other four-year	740	1,674	44	n.a.	n.a.	n.a.	n.a.
Two-year	340	893	38	n.a.	n.a.	3.6	n.a.
Private, total	965	2,133	45	n.a.	n.a.	n.a.	n.a.
Universities	30	280	11	n.a.	n.a.	n.a.	n.a.
Other four-year	--	--	--	--	--	--	--
Two-year	985	1,853	50	n.a.	n.a.	n.a.	n.a.

II. Vocational enrollment

	Women	Total	Women as Percent of Total
A. Fiscal year 1974 enrollment in state-approved postsecondary, total (unduplicated)[6]	n.a.	6,442	40†[7]
Occupations:			
Trade and industry		261	13
Technical		1,255	8
Home economics (gainful)		244	84
Health		757	92
Office		3,437	62
Distributive		259	26
Other		189	n.a.
B. Fall 1973 full- and part-time enrollment, public and private (nonprofit; nondegree credit)	1,385	2,170	64
C. Calendar year 1972 apprenticeships, total numbers[9]	4	253	2
D. Fiscal year 1974 MDTA training[10]	n.a.		
Institutional		300	36
JOBS Optional/On-the-Job Training		n.a.	22‡

Expenditures, fiscal year 1974[8]

State/Local	Federal
3.7	.2

(for II.A)

Federal Obligations, Fiscal Year 1974[11]

	Federal Obligations Fiscal Year 1974[11]
Institutional	.9
JOBS Optional/On-the-Job Training	.1

71

level, although when nondegree-credit enrollment is included, the representation of the sexes is just about a draw. In vocational programs overall (if the national percentages hold in this state, a circumstance that cannot be determined because of lacking data) women are possibly underrepresented (see Table 2.4). However, about $1 million of federal tax-derived funds in 1974 were used under the manpower programs to train almost twice as many young men as young women.

FLORIDA

Enrollment

As Table 3.5 indicates, girls in 1973 were just about half the high school graduatss, yet were only 41 percent of the full-time degree-credit undergraduate enrollment in the state and less than 40 percent at several of the top-ranking research universities. At the public two-year colleges women were also outnumbered by about 3:2. Of the 9,500 bachelor's degrees received by Florida women in 1972, about 45 percent were in the field of education.

Women were 47 percent of enrollment in nondegree-credit programs in Florida higher education. Of the 5,955 apprenticeships reported to the Equal Employment Opportunity Commission, 4, or less than .06 percent, were women. Under the fiscal year 1974 federally funded manpower training programs, women in Florida were almost half of those enrolled.

Funding from Taxes

Almost one-third of the fiscal year 1972 state tax funds appropriated for higher education went to the research universities and associated medical facilities; almost three-quarters of the federal fiscal year 1973 obligations to Florida higher education went to these same institutions. At the University of Florida and University of Miami, women are outnumbered by 3:2 in undergraduate enrollment. Women in 1972 received 18 percent of doctorates granted by Florida institutions, and, among first professional degrees, 7 percent of the degrees in medicine and 5 percent in law. Few young women benefit from the approximately $20 million awarded from state tax funds to the medical facilities associated with the universities, nor do they to any great extent share in the capitation support for Florida residents, funded at $4.2 million in 1974-75 for M.D. training at the University of Miami Medical School.

In addition, 1973-74 business gifts of $4.9 million and foundation grants of $4.4 million earned their donors tax reductions while contributing toward strengthened faculty, facilities, and research activities of the research universities. All taxpayers thus involuntarily subsidized the education of about three young men for every two young women, since the taxes not paid by the donors must be made up by the rest of the taxpayers.

The $33 million in federal, state, and local funds expended in fiscal year 1974 for postsecondary vocational education may have been more equally shared by the sexes, although national data on percentage enrollment by sex by program indicates a majority of men (see Table 2.4). Other programs with state data available, such as apprenticeship and on-the-job training, strongly favor young men.

ILLINOIS

Enrollment

As Table 3.6 indicates, girls in 1973 were slightly more than half the high school graduates, yet were only 45 percent of full-time, degree-credit undergraduate enrollment in the state and only 38 percent of enrollment in the top-ranking research universities. Women were 53 percent of enrollment in "other four-year" public institutions, often specializing in teacher training. Of the 20,000 bachelor's degrees received by Illinois women in 1972, 43 percent were in education. At the public two-year colleges women were outnumbered by almost 3:2.

Women were 48 percent of enrollment in nondegree-credit programs in Illinois higher education. Of the 11,396 apprenticeships reported in 1972 to the Equal Employment Opportunity Commission, 27, or .2 percent, were women. Under the federally funded manpower training programs, women in Illinois in fiscal year 1974 were 60 percent of those enrolled in institutional training.

Funding from Taxes

No breakdown of state funds to the University of Illinois campuses is available, but almost three-quarters of all federal obligations to higher education in Illinois for fiscal year 1973 went to the research universities and associated medical centers. In fiscal year 1975, grants to institutions for increased enrollment of Illinois residents in medical, nursing, dental, and similar fields were appropriated from state tax funds in the amount of $17 million. At the

TABLE 3.5

Opportunities for Women in Education Beyond High School in Florida

	Enrollment in Postsecondary Institutions			Financial Support (in millions of dollars)			
				Tax-Exempt Funds, 1973-74[1]		Tax Funds	
	Women	Total	Women as Percent of Total	Private Business	Private Foundations	State Tax Funds, Fiscal Year 1972[2]	Federal Obligations, Fiscal Year 1973[3]
1973 high school graduates[4]	41,002	81,773	50				
I. Academic (degree credit) enrollment							
Fall 1973 full-time undergraduate enrollment, public and private (nonprofit), state total							
A. Research universities, *[5] total	58,691	143,532	41	n.a.	n.a.	247.5	84.0
Public: University of Florida	17,178	39,877	43	4.9	4.4	63.9[a]	61.9
Florida State University	6,970	17,788	39	1.8	1.8	33.2	25.1
	7,245	14,141	51	n.a.	n.a.	30.7	8.9
Private: University of Miami	2,963	7,948	37	3.1	2.6	b	27.9
B. Excluding research universities							
Public, total	33,305	81,202	41	n.a.	n.a.	n.a.	n.a.
Universities	1,898	4,000	47	n.a.	n.a.	n.a.	n.a.
Other four-year	11,734	29,176	40	n.a.	n.a.	n.a.	n.a.
Two-year	19,673	48,026	41	n.a.	n.a.	85.4	n.a.
Private, total	8,208	22,453	36	n.a.	n.a.	n.a.	n.a.
Universities	--	--	--	--	--	--	--
Other four-year	7,852	21,801	36	n.a.	n.a.	n.a.	n.a.
Two-year	356	652	55	n.a.	n.a.	n.a.	n.a.

				Expenditures, fiscal year 1974[8]	
				State/Local	Federal
II. Vocational enrollment				29.8	3.5
A. Fiscal year 1974 enrollment in state-approved postsecondary, total (unduplicated)[6]	n.a.	104,950	40+7		
Occupations:					
Trade and industry		16,729	13		
Technical		26,061	8		
Home economics (gainful)		1,799	84		
Health		18,839	92		
Office		23,391	62		
Distributive		14,578	26		
Other		3,553	n.a.		
B. Fall 1973 full- and part-time enrollment public and private (nonprofit; nondegree credit)	16,792	35,907	47		
C. Calendar year 1972 apprenticeships, total numbers[9]	4	5,955	.06		
D. Fiscal year 1974 MDTA training[10]				Federal Obligations, Fiscal Year, 1974[11]	
Institutional		2,500	48	8.6	
JOBS Optional/On-the-Job Training		n.a.	22‡	.9	

aAdditional appropriation: University of Florida Health Center, $14.1 million; University of Southern Florida Medical Center, $2.4 million.

bUniversity of Miami Medical School, $5.6 million.

TABLE 3.6

Opportunities for Women in Education Beyond High School in Illinois

	Enrollment in Postsecondary Institutions			Financial Support (in millions of dollars)			
				Tax-Exempt Funds, 1973-74[1]		Tax Funds	
						State Tax Funds, Fiscal Year 1972[2]	Federal Obligations, Fiscal Year 1973[3]
	Women	Total	Women as Percent of Total	Private Business	Private Foundations		
1973 high school graduates[4]	69,161	135,735	51				
I. Academic (degree credit) enrollment							
Fall 1973 full-time undergraduate enrollment, public and private (nonprofit), state total	104,410	234,098	45	n.a.	n.a.	470.4	169.5
A. Research universities,*[5] total	13,605	35,366	38	9.6	11.4	n.a.	109.1c
Public: University of Illinois, Urbana	9,846	24,682	40	4.1	2.0	a	42.2
Private: Northwestern University	2,887	6,671	43	2.6	3.4		20.9
University of Chicago	702	2,055	34	2.0	5.9	b	40.0
Illinois Institute of Technology	170	1,958	9	.9	.1		6.0
B. Excluding research universities							
Public, total	63,547	140,624	45	n.a.	n.a.	n.a.	n.a.
Universities	22,243	52,231	42	n.a.	n.a.	n.a.	n.a.
Other four-year	23,213	44,065	53	n.a.	n.a.	n.a.	n.a.
Two-year	18,091	44,328	41	n.a.	n.a.	55.1	n.a.
Private, total	27,258	58,108	47	n.a.	n.a.	n.a.	n.a.
Universities	5,657	12,158	46	n.a.	n.a.	n.a.	n.a.
Other four-year	19,501	41,457	47	n.a.	n.a.	n.a.	n.a.
Two-year	2,100	4,493	47	n.a.	n.a.	n.a.	n.a.

Expenditures, fiscal year 1974[8]

	State/Local	Federal
	25.0	3.7

II. Vocational enrollment

A. Fiscal year 1974 enrollment in state-approved postsecondary, total (unduplicated)[6] n.a. 81,469 40+[7]

Occupations:

Trade and industry	16,740	13
Technical	9,082	8
Home economics (gainful)	3,146	84
Health	11,283	92
Office	30,250	62
Distributive	5,850	26
Other	5,118	n.a.

B. Fall 1973 full- and part-time enrollment, public and private (nonprofit; nondegree credit) 34,813 72,706 48

C. Calendar year 1972 apprenticeships, total numbers[9] 27 11,396 .2

Federal Obligations, Fiscal Year 1974[11]

D. Fiscal year 1974 MDTA training[10]

Institutional	4,700	60	15.3
JOBS Optional/On-the-Job Training	n.a.	22‡	4.0

a $158 million appropriation covers all University of Illinois campuses.

b Appropriation: $6 million University of Chicago Medical College.

c Plus $12.5 million, University of Illinois Medical Center.

research institutions where women are outnumbered by 3:2, tax-derived funds serve to enhance the research and teaching capabilities of faculty. Women in 1972 received 15 percent of doctorates granted by Illinois institutions, and, among first-professional degrees, 7 percent of the degrees in medicine and 6 percent in law.

The research universities received gifts in 1973-74 from corporate donors of $9.6 million and an additional $11.4 million in foundation grants. These gifts earned their donors tax reductions, while contributing toward strengthened faculty, facilities, and research activities of the recipient institutions. Since women are outnumbered 3:2 at the research universities, all taxpayers thus involuntarily subsidized the education of three young men for every two young women, since the taxes not paid by the donors must be made up by the rest of the taxpayers.

The $29 million of federal, state, and local funds expended in fiscal year 1974 for Illinois postsecondary vocational education at least slightly benefit more men than women, if national percentages hold (see Table 2.4). In fiscal year 1974, unlike earlier years, more young women in Illinois participated in manpower program institutional training, and thus received the lion's share of the $15 million federal obligations in that year, although presumably receiving only a small share of the $4 million devoted to on-the-job training.

KANSAS

Enrollment

As Table 3.7 indicates, girls in 1973 were just about half the Kansas high school graduates, yet were only 43 percent of full-time degree-credit undergraduate enrollment in the state and only 42 percent of enrollment in the top-ranking research universities. At the public two-year colleges women were outnumbered by 3:2. Of the 5,400 bachelor's degrees received by Kansas women in 1972, 42 percent were in education.

Women were 51 percent of nondegree-credit program enrollment in Kansas higher education in 1973. Of the 448 apprenticeships reported in 1972 to the Equal Employment Opportunity Commission, none went to women. Under the federally funded manpower training programs, women in Kansas in fiscal year 1974 were only about one-fifth of those in institutional and on-the-job training.

Funding from Taxes

Almost two-thirds of the fiscal year 1973 state tax funds appropriated for operating expenses of higher education went to the research universities and associated medical facilities; about 75 percent of the fiscal year 1973 federal obligations to Kansas higher education went to these same institutions. Women in 1972 received 13 percent of doctorates granted by Kansas institutions, and, among first-professional degrees, 6 percent of the degrees in medicine and 3 percent in law.

Since the research universities also received $800,000 in corporate gifts and $1 million in foundation grants, their faculty, facilities, and research activities were once more enhanced. All taxpayers thus involuntarily subsidized the education of almost three young men for every two young women, since these gifts earned tax-exemptions for their donors; taxes not paid by such donors must be made up by the rest of the taxpayers.

The $7.0 million in federal, state, and local funds expended in fiscal year 1974 for postsecondary vocational education appears to have been used to train more than three young men for every two young women if national percentages hold (see Table 2.4). Federal and state funds used for major apprenticeship programs in Kansas benefited no young women. The $4 million of federal funds obligated in fiscal year 1974 for institutional and on-the-job training were used to train about four young men for every young woman.

MASSACHUSETTS

Enrollment

Among the states, Massachusetts has long been a leader in education. However, the early advantage in establishment of private higher education has ultimately worked to the disadvantage of young women residents. The national or research universities have attracted young men from all parts of the nation, and indeed, in graduate study, of the world. Thus as Table 3.8 shows, women do not share equally in the abundance of riches that is the Massachusetts educational system.

In 1972 girls were just about half of all high school graduates; in 1973 they were 47 percent of full-time degree-credit undergraduate enrollment in the state, but only 41 percent of enrollment in the research universities. Women were a majority of enrollment (52 percent) in the "other four-year" public institutions, the former state teachers colleges. Of the 15,000 bachelor's degrees received by Massachusetts women in 1972, almost one-third (4,700) were in education. At the public two-year colleges women were 44 percent of enrollment.

TABLE 3.7.

Opportunities for Women in Education Beyond High School in Kansas

| | Enrollment in Postsecondary Institutions | | | Financial Support (in millions of dollars) | | | |
| | | | | Tax-Exempt Funds, 1973-74[1] | | Tax Funds Fiscal Year 1973 | |
	Women	Total	Women as Percent of Total	Private Business	Private Foundations	State Tax Funds[2]	Federal Obligations[3]
1973 high school graduates [4]	16,831	33,941	50				
I. Academic (degree credit) enrollment							
Fall 1973 full-time undergraduate enrollment, public and private (nonprofit), state total	28,615	67,162	43	n.a.	n.a.	93.1	37.7
A. Research universities,*[5] total	10,703	25,229	42	.8	1.0	48.5	28.6
Public: Kansas State University	4,989	12,069	41	.2	.2	24.2	8.2
University of Kansas	5,714	13,160	43	.6	.8	24.3a	20.4
Private	---	---	---	---	---	---	---
B. Excluding research universities							
Public, total	12,729	31,272	41	n.a.	n.a.	n.a.	n.a.
Universities	2,363	5,993	39	n.a.	n.a.	n.a.	n.a.
Other four-year	6,072	14,039	43	n.a.	n.a.	n.a.	n.a.
Two-year	4,294	11,240	38	n.a.	n.a.	3.9	n.a.
Private, total	5,183	10,661	49	n.a.	n.a.	n.a.	n.a.
Universities	---	---	---	---	---	---	---
Other four-year	4,628	9,618	49	n.a.	n.a.	n.a.	n.a.
Two-year	555	1,043	53	n.a.	n.a.	n.a.	n.a.

			Expenditures, fiscal year 1974[8]	
			State/Local	Federal
			5.5	1.5

II. Vocational enrollment

				Federal Obligations, Fiscal Year 1974[11]
A. Fiscal year 1974 enrollment in state-approved postsecondary, total (unduplicated)[6]	n.a.	8,638	40†[7]	
Occupations:				
Trade and industry		3,871	13	
Technical		439	8	
Home economics (gainful)		12	84	
Health		1,165	92	
Office		2,165	62	
Distributive		413	26	
Other		566	n.a.	
B. Fall 1973 full- and part-time enrollment, public and private (nonprofit; nondegree credit)	2,577	5,089	51	
C. Calendar year 1972 apprenticeships, total numbers[9]	0	448	0	
D. Fiscal year 1974 MDTA training[10]				
Institutional		1,400	20	3.1
JOBS Optional/On-the-Job Training		n.a.	22‡	.9

[a]Additional appropriation: $11.6 million, University of Kansas Medical Center.

TABLE 3.8

Opportunities for Women in Education Beyond High School in Massachusetts

| | Enrollment in Postsecondary Institutions | | | Financial Support (in millions of dollars) | | | |
| | | | | Tax-Exempt Funds, 1973-74[1] | | Tax Funds | |
	Women	Total	Women as Percent of Total	Private Business	Private Foundations	State Tax Funds, Fiscal Year 1972[2]	Federal Obligations, Fiscal Year 1973[3]
1973 high school graduates[a4]	33,878	67,487	50[b]				
I. Academic (degree credit) enrollment							
Fall 1973 full-time undergraduate enrollment, public and private (nonprofit), state total	85,168	182,474	47	n.a.	n.a.	130.2	281.0
A. Research universities,*[5] total	19,568	47,247	41	18.2	33.2	n.a.	234.9
Public: University of Massachusetts, Amherst	7,876	17,911	44	.5	.6	c	11.8
Private: Harvard University	1,593	6,247	26	9.4	17.7	n.a.	61.4
Massachusetts Institute of Technology	481	4,008	12	7.3	9.1	n.a.	125.5
Boston University	6,619	12,595	52	.5	4.0	n.a.	20.1
Brandeis University	1,189	2,481	48	.1	1.1	n.a.	5.9
Tufts University	1,810	4,005	45	.4	.7	n.a.	10.2
B. Excluding research universities							
Public, total	28,332	56,742	50	n.a.	n.a.	n.a.	n.a.
Universities	2,651	5,689	47	n.a.	n.a.	n.a.	n.a.
Other four-year	20,082	38,388	52	n.a.	n.a.	n.a.	n.a.
Two-year	5,599	12,665	44	n.a.	n.a.	18.6	n.a.
Private, total	37,268	78,485	47	n.a.	n.a.	n.a.	n.a.
Universities	8,304	22,258	37	n.a.	n.a.	n.a.	n.a.
Other four-year	23,385	47,052	50	n.a.	n.a.	n.a.	n.a.
Two-year	5,579	9,175	61	n.a.	n.a.	n.a.	n.a.

Expenditures, fiscal year 1974[8]

	State/Local	Federal
	12.5	2.2

II. Vocational enrollment

A. Fiscal year 1974 enrollment in state-approved postsecondary, total (unduplicated)[6] — n.a. — 13,713 — 40[+7]

Occupations:

Trade and industry	1,500	13
Technical	2,734	8
Home economics (gainful)	602	84
Health	4,374	92
Office	6,127	62
Distributive	839	26
Other	537	n.a.

B. Fall 1973 full- and part-time enrollment; public and private (nonprofit; nondegree credit) — 11,267 — 23,408 — 48

C. Calendar year 1972 apprenticeships, total numbers[9] — 13 — 3,133 — .4

		Federal Obligations, Fiscal Year 1974[11]
D. Fiscal year 1974 MDTA training[10]		
Institutional	2,900	53 — 7.4
JOBS Optional/On-the-Job Training	n.a.	22[‡] — 3.0

[a] 1973 data n.a.; 1972 graduates.

[b] Distribution estimated by Office of Education.

[c] $58.6 million appropriation covers all University of Massachusetts campuses and Medical School.

Women were 48 percent of nondegree-credit program enrollment in Massachusetts higher education in 1973. Of the 3,133
apprenticeships reported to the Equal Employment Opportunity Commission in 1972, 13, or .4 percent, were women. Women, however,
were slightly over half of enrollment in institutional training under
the federally funded manpower training.

Funding from Taxes

No breakdown of state funds among the University of Massachusetts campuses is provided, but 84 percent of fiscal year 1973
federal obligations went to the research universities. In addition
these same institutions received in 1973-74 about $18 million in
corporate gifts and $33 million in foundation grants. Since such
donors receive tax-exemptions, all taxpayers involuntarily subsidized the education of almost three young men for every two young
women; taxes not paid by the donors must be made up by the rest of
the taxpayers. Women in 1972 received 17 percent of doctorates
granted by Massachusetts institutions, and, among first-professional
degrees, 13 percent of the degrees in medicine and 10 percent in law.
In fiscal year 1975, medical, dental, and nursing scholarships
were funded at $500,000; an additional $500,000 was appropriated
to assist Massachusetts residents attending medical and dental
schools in other New England states, under a regional program.
Given the sex distribution of medical and dental degrees nationwide,
a very small portion of these funds will benefit women. Massachusetts has recently joined the growing number of states in which
state aid to private institutions may be appropriated from public
funds. It thus becomes all the more essential that such funds be
even-handedly utilized by the recipient institutions.
The $15 million in federal, state, and local funds expended in
fiscal year 1974 for postsecondary vocational education may have
been more equally distributed since women are almost equally represented in nondegree programs. However, if Massachusetts follows
the national trend, women are less-well-represented in overall
noncollegiate postsecondary vocational education (see Table 2.4).
Federal and state funds used for major apprenticeship programs in
Massachusetts were almost entirely to the benefit of young men.
While young women predominated in the institutional training program
for which $7.4 in federal funds were obligated in fiscal year 1974,
they were presumably outnumbered by about 4:1 in the $3 million
on-the-job training program.

MICHIGAN

Enrollment

Women in 1973 were just half the graduates of Michigan high schools, yet only 44 percent of full-time degree-credit undergraduate enrollment in the state. In contrast to the pattern of enrollment in other states studied, women were a higher percent of enrollment in the research universities, which in this state are public institutions. On closer examination of fields of specialization of baccalaureate recipients however, it appears that in 1972 about 40 percent of degrees received by women were in education, nursing, and health professions at the University of Michigan, for example. Thus the higher percentage of women in research universities in this state does not reflect any real difference in the pattern of enrollment. About one-third of the 17,000 bachelor's degrees received by Michigan women in 1972 were in the field of education. In public two-year colleges women are outnumbered about 3:2.

Women were 45 percent of enrollment in nondegree-credit programs in Michigan higher education. Of the 9,300 apprentice-ships reported to the Equal Employment Opportunity Commission in 1972, 12, or .1 percent, were women. Under the federally funded manpower training programs, women in Michigan were 47 percent of those in institutional training.

Funding from Taxes

Half the state tax funds appropriated for higher education went to the research universities, as well as almost 80 percent of all federal obligations to Michigan higher education. Although women in Michigan are better represented at these institutions than is the case in many other states, there is unequal representation of the sexes, especially in fields not traditionally associated with women, as was noted above. Federal tax exemption for gifts and grants by corporations or foundations, as well as the Michigan state law permitting private and corporate donors to take credit against state income tax for contributions to higher education, means that other taxpayers must pay higher taxes to compensate. Because of sex discriminatory enrollment in Michigan higher education, all taxpayers are thus involuntarily subsidizing the education of more young men than young women.

Although we are concerned here with undergraduates, awards under contracts with private institutions awarding dental medicine

TABLE 3.9

Opportunities for Women in Education Beyond High School in Michigan

	Enrollment in Postsecondary Institutions			Financial Support (in millions of dollars)			
				Tax-Exempt Funds, 1973-74[1]		Tax Funds	
						State Tax Funds, Fiscal Year 1972[2]	Federal Obligations, Fiscal Year 1973[3]
	Women	Total	Women as Percent of Total	Private Business	Private Foundations		
1973 high school graduates[a4]	63,580	126,409	50				
I. Academic (degree credit) enrollment							
Fall 1973 full-time undergraduate enrollment, public and private (nonprofit), state total	86,949	197,970	44	n.a.	n.a.	379.4	122.7
A. Research universities,*[5] total	29,166	63,245	46	11.7	10.7	189.2	95.3
Public: University of Michigan (main campus)	8,267	18,707	44	8.6	8.1	72.7	56.9
Michigan State University	13,997	29,520	47	1.8	1.6	65.3	25.5
Wayne State University	6,902	15,018	46	1.3	1.0	51.2	12.9
Private	---	---	---	---	---	---	---
B. Excluding research universities							
Public, total	43,379	100,338	43	n.a.	n.a.	n.a.	n.a.
Universities	1,609	3,764	43	n.a.	n.a.	n.a.	n.a.
Other four-year	29,448	66,461	44	n.a.	n.a.	n.a.	n.a.
Two-year	12,322	30,113	41	n.a.	n.a.	52.7	n.a.
Private, total	14,404	34,387	42	n.a.	n.a.	n.a.	n.a.
Universities	1,217	3,476	35	n.a.	n.a.	n.a.	n.a.
Other four-year	12,130	28,931	42	n.a.	n.a.	n.a.	n.a.
Two-year	1,057	1,980	53	n.a.	n.a.	n.a.	n.a.

	Expenditures, fiscal year 1974[8]	
	State/Local	Federal
II. Vocational enrollment	20,6	3.5

A. Fiscal year 1974 enrollment in state-approved postsecondary, total (unduplicated)[6]	n.a.	67,106	40[+7]
Occupations:			
Trade and industry		16,524	13
Technical		11,109	8
Home economics (gainful)		533	84
Health		12,739	92
Office		22,294	62
Distributive		2,770	26
Other		1,137	n.a.
B. Fall 1973 full- and part-time enrollment, public and private (nonprofit; nondegree credit)	33,698	74,231	45
C. Calendar year 1972 apprenticeships, total numbers[9]	12	9,305	.1

			Federal Obligations Fiscal Year 1974[11]
D. Fiscal year 1974 MDTA training[10]			
Institutional	4,500	47	14.8
JOBS Optional/On-the-Job Training	n.a.	22[‡]	3.4

[a] 1973 data not available; 1972 graduates.

degrees ($2,400 each) and law degrees ($1,200 each) to Michigan
residents were funded at about $600,000 in 1974-75; another $2 million of 1974-75 funding provided $200 for each associate degree and
$400 for each bachelor's and master's degree. Since women in 1972
received only 8 percent of law degrees and none of the dentistry degrees, and received about 39 percent and 40 percent, respectively,
of bachelor's and master's degrees awarded by private institutions,
tax-derived funds are being used in a discriminatory fashion. Similar criticism may be made regarding the obligation of public credit
authorized in January 1975 for the issuance of tax-exempt bonds for
construction of academic facilities of Michigan private institutions.

The $24 million federal, state, and local funds expended in
fiscal year 1974 for Michigan postsecondary vocational education
likewise benefits more men than women, if national percentages
represent a good approximation of in-state enrollment distribution
(see Table 2.4). Federal and state funds used for major apprenticeship programs in Michigan benefit young men almost exclusively.
More men than women benefited from the $15 million of fiscal year
1974 federal obligations for institutional training under manpower
programs, and women received only a small share of the $3 million
devoted to on-the-job training.

MISSISSIPPI

Enrollment

As Table 3.10 indicates, women were slightly over half the
1973 Mississippi high school graduates and 47 percent of full-time,
degree-credit undergraduate enrollment in the state, yet were only
35 percent of enrollment at top-ranking Mississippi State University.
Women were 55 percent of enrollment at "other four-year" public
institutions, which have concentrated on teacher training. Of the
4,300 bachelor's degrees earned by Mississippi women in 1972, almost exactly half were in education.

Women were 44 percent of enrollment in nondegree-credit
programs in Mississippi higher education in 1973. Of the 814 apprenticeships reported in 1972 to the Equal Employment Opportunity
Commission, 2, or .2 percent, went to women. Under the federally
funded manpower training programs, women in Mississippi were
outnumbered 3:2 in institutional training.

Funding from Taxes

About one-fifth of state tax funds appropriated for operating
expenses of state higher education went to the research university,

Mississippi State, and its related medical facilities; almost one-third of federal obligations for fiscal year 1973 to all Mississippi higher education went to the same institution. Women in 1972 received 18 percent of doctorates awarded by Mississippi institutions, and, among first-professional degrees, 10 percent of degrees in medicine and 4 percent in law.

The $9 million of federal, state, and local funds expended in fiscal year 1974 for Mississippi postsecondary vocational education appears to benefit substantially more men than women, if Mississippi follows national percentages (see Table 2.4). Young women were virtually excluded from major apprenticeship programs using federal and state funds. The $6 million of federal funds obligated in fiscal year 1974 for institutional and on-the-job training was used to train more than three young men for every two young women.

NEVADA

Enrollment

Women in 1973 were half the Nevada high school graduates, yet only 38 percent of 1973 enrollment in higher education in the state. Nearly one-third of Nevada students left the state for undergraduate study in 1968, the year of the latest published migration study, but men outnumbered women 3:2 among such outmigrants. In public two-year colleges women were less than one-third of enrollment.

Women were 40 percent of enrollment in nondegree-credit programs of Nevada higher education. Of the 845 apprenticeships reported to the Equal Employment Opportunity Commission in 1972, 4, or .5 percent, were women. Under the federally funded man-power training programs, women in Nevada were less than one-third of those in institutional training.

Funding from Taxes

About $21 million in fiscal year 1973 state tax fund appropriations and $7 million of federal obligations to state higher education contributes to the undergraduate education of three young men for every two young women so aided. Women are equally underrepresented in Nevada vocational education, supported by $600,000 in state, local, and federal funds, and are almost excluded from major apprenticeship programs benefiting from public funds. Women receive less than one-third of the $1.4 million of federal obligations for institutional and on-the-job training programs.

TABLE 3.10

Opportunities for Women in Education Beyond High School in Mississippi

| | Enrollment in Postsecondary Institutions | | | Financial Support (in millions of dollars) | | | |
| | | | | Tax-Exempt Funds, 1973-74[1] | | Tax Funds, Fiscal Year 1973 | |
	Women	Total	Women as Percent of Total	Private Business	Private Foundations	State Tax Funds[2]	Federal Obligations[3]
1973 high school graduates [4]	13,479	26,128	52				
I. Academic (degree credit) enrollment							
Fall 1973 full-time undergraduate enrollment, public and private (nonprofit), state total	25,651	54,299	47	n.a.	n.a.	97.0	32.9
A. Research universities*[5]							
Public: Mississippi State University	2,803	8,074	35	n.a.	n.a.	11.0[a]	10.3
Private	--	--	--	--	--	--	--
B. Excluding research universities							
Public, total	19,525	39,721	49	n.a.	n.a.	n.a.	n.a.
Universities	2,491	5,998	42	n.a.	n.a.	n.a.	n.a.
Other four-year	10,864	19,817	55	n.a.	n.a.	22.6	n.a.
Two-year	6,170	13,906	44	n.a.	n.a.	n.a.	n.a.
Private, total	3,323	6,504	51	n.a.	n.a.	n.a.	n.a.
Universities	--	--	--	--	--	--	--
Other four-year	2,901	5,631	52	n.a.	n.a.	n.a.	n.a.
Two-year	422	873	48	n.a.	n.a.	n.a.	n.a.

| | | | Expenditures, fiscal year 1974[8] | |
| | | | State/Local | Federal |

II. Vocational enrollment

| | | | 7.8 | .8 |

A. Fiscal year 1974 enrollment in state-approved postsecondary, total (unduplicated)[6]

| | n.a. | 10,623 | 40+[7] |

Occupations:

Trade and industry	4,482	13
Technical	1,328	8
Home economics (gainful)	94	84
Health	1,974	92
Office	1,874	62
Distributive	537	26
Other	339	n.a.

B. Fall 1973 full- and part-time enrollment, public and private (nonprofit; nondegree credit)

| | 4,041 | 9,272 | 44 |

C. Calendar year 1972 apprenticeships, total numbers[9]

| | 2 | 814 | .2 |

D. Fiscal year 1974 MDTA training[10]

			Federal Obligations, Fiscal Year 1974[11]
Institutional	1,600	38	4.6
JOBS Optional/On-the-Job Training	n.a.	22‡	.9

[a] Additional appropriation: $9.5 million, University of Mississippi Medical School and Hospital; $1.2 million, nursing programs, University of Mississippi, University of Southern Mississippi, Mississippi State College for Women.

TABLE 3.11

Opportunities for Women in Education Beyond High School in Nevada

| | Enrollment in Postsecondary Institutions | | | Financial Support (in millions of dollars) | | | |
| | | | | Tax-Exempt Funds, 1973-74[1] | | Tax Funds Fiscal Year 1973 | |
	Women	Total	Women as Percent of Total	Private Business	Private Foundations	State Tax Funds[2]	Federal Obligations[3]
1973 high school graduates[4]	3,198	6,414	50				
I. Academic (degree credit) enrollment							
Fall 1973 full-time undergraduate enrollment, public and private (nonprofit), state total	3,619	9,595	38	n.a.	n.a.	20.6	6.6
Public, total	3,592	9,519	38	n.a.	.5	n.a.	n.a.
Universities	1,846	4,549	40	n.a.	n.a.	n.a.	n.a.
Other four-year	1,281	3,425	37	n.a.	n.a.	n.a.	n.a.
Two-year	465	1,545	30	n.a.	n.a.	1.1	n.a.
Private, total	27	76	36	n.a.	n.a.	n.a.	n.a.
Universities	--	--	--	--	--	--	--
Other four-year	27	76	36	n.a.	n.a.	n.a.	n.a.
Two-year	--	--	--	--	--	--	--

II. Vocational enrollment

	Women	Total	Women as Percent of Total	Expenditures, fiscal year 1974[8] State/Local	Federal
A. Fiscal year 1974 enrollment in state-approved postsecondary, total (unduplicated)[6]	n.a.	6,342	40[7]	.5	.1
Occupations:					
Trade and industry		2,519	13		
Technical		1,472	8		
Home economics (gainful)		549	84		
Health		1,981	92		
Office		a	62		
Distributive		1,083	26		
Other		n.a.	n.a.		
B. Fall 1973 full- and part-time enrollment, public and private (nonprofit; nondegree credit)	1,735	4,344	40		
C. Calendar year 1972 apprenticeships, total numbers[9]	4	845	.5		

	Total	Women as Percent of Total	Federal Obligations Fiscal Year 1974[11]
D. Fiscal year 1974 MDTA training[10]			
Institutional	500	32	1.2
JOBS Optional/On-the-Job Training	n.a.	22[‡]	.2

aShown as 4,217, apparent error in listing.

NEW JERSEY

Enrollment

Among New Jersey high school graduates in 1973, girls were 51 percent of the total. Yet in the state's research universities women were only 40 percent of enrollment--44 percent at Rutgers and 27 percent at Princeton. Although New Jersey sent about half its students in undergraduate higher education to colleges out of state in 1968 (the latest published migration study by sex), men were "exported" rather than women, again in a 3:2 ratio. However, women were 53 percent of enrollment in the "other four-year" institutions, which have concentrated on teacher training. At public two-year colleges women were only 43 percent.

Women were better represented numerically as 50 percent of occupational programs of New Jersey higher education in 1973 and 55 percent of fiscal year 1974 institutional trainees under the federally funded manpower training programs. However, of the 2,800 apprenticeships reported to the Equal Employment Opportunity Commission, only 19, or .7 percent, went to women.

Funding from Taxes

About one-fourth of fiscal year 1973 state tax funds appropriated for higher education operating expenses and over half of total federal obligations to New Jersey institutions of higher education went to the two research universities which enroll about 16 percent of state undergraduates. Women in 1972 received 11 percent of all doctorates awarded by New Jersey institutions, and, among first-professional degrees, 5 percent of degrees in medicine and 8 percent in law.

In addition to appropriations for operating expenses of public higher education, competitive scholarships were funded at $7.5 million in 1974-75, of which $5.5 million is assigned to private institutions. In addition, incentive grants for scholarship holders and tuition aid grants based on financial need to students attending higher-tuition institutions, funded at $6 million in 1974-75, effectively exclude students at state colleges, where women represent 53 percent of enrollment. (Fifth-three percent of all New Jersey women undergraduates in 1973 attended public "other four-year" institutions.) Contracts with private colleges and universities "to maintain and preserve these educational resources"* were funded at $8 million in

---

*Education Commission of the States, Higher Education in the States (Denver, 1975), p. 14.

TABLE 3.12

Opportunities for Women in Education Beyond High School in New Jersey

| | Enrollment in Postsecondary Institutions | | | Financial Support (in millions of dollars) | | | |
| | | | | Tax-Exempt Funds, 1973-74[1] | | Tax Funds Fiscal Year 1973 | |
	Women	Total	Women as Percent of Total	Private Business	Private Foundations	State Tax Funds[2]	Federal Obligations[3]
1973 high school graduates[4]	46,562	91,629	51				
I. Academic (degree credit) enrollment							
Fall 1973 full-time undergraduate enrollment, public and private (nonprofit), state total	57,284	122,992	46	n.a.		236.3	60.3
A. Research universities,*[5] total	7,873	19,485	40	3.6	4.9	64.8b	32.0c
Public: Rutgers University	6,748	15,267	44	2.0	.6	64.8a	15.7
Private: Princeton University	1,125	4,218	27	1.6	4.3	n.a.	16.3
B. Excluding research universities							
Public, total	35,276	71,112	50	n.a.	n.a.	n.a.	n.a.
Universities	2,188	5,332	41	n.a.	n.a.	n.a.	n.a.
Other four-year	24,690	46,450	53	n.a.	n.a.	n.a.	n.a.
Two-year	8,398	19,330	43	n.a.	n.a.	29.5	n.a.
Private, total	14,135	32,395	44	n.a.	n.a.	n.a.	n.a.
Universities	1,822	4,438	41	n.a.	n.a.	n.a.	n.a.
Other four-year	11,251	25,708	44	n.a.	n.a.	n.a.	n.a.
Two-year	1,062	2,249	47	n.a.	n.a.	n.a.	n.a.

		State/Local 3.2	Federal 2.1	Federal Obligations, Fiscal Year 1974[11]
		Expenditures, fiscal year 1974[8]		
II.	Vocational enrollment			
A.	Fiscal year 1974 enrollment in state-approved postsecondary, total (unduplicated)[6]	n.a.	30,733	40+[7]
	Occupations:			
	Trade and industry		3,036	13
	Technical		8,729	8
	Home economics (gainful)		123	84
	Health		9,401	92
	Office		6,910	62
	Distributive		2,537	26
	Other		2	n.a.
B.	Fall 1973 full- and part-time enrollment, public and private (nonprofit; nondegree credit)	10,639	21,184	50
C.	Calendar year 1972 apprenticeships, total numbers[9]	19	2,838	.7
D.	Fiscal year 1974 MDTA training[10]			
	Institutional	5,100	55	11.8
	JOBS Optional/On-the-Job Training	n.a.	22‡	3.0

[a] Additional appropriation: $34.8 million, New Jersey College of Medicine and Dentistry.
[b] Includes all campus units.
[c] Federal obligation: $11.8 million, New Jersey College of Medicine and Dentistry.

1974-75, with varying amounts for upper- and lower-class students, and for additional students. Public credit obligation, through issuance of tax-exempt bonds for construction, is also authorized. Women were only 42 percent of enrollment at all private institutions, and just over 33 percent at all private universities in New Jersey.

Corporate gifts of $3.6 million and grants of $4.9 million from general welfare foundations earned tax reductions for the donors; all other taxpayers thus involuntarily subsidize the education of more young men than young women, since the taxes not paid by the donors must be made up by the rest of the taxpayers.

The $5 million in federal, state, and local funds expended in fiscal year 1974 for postsecondary vocational education may also have benefited more men than women, if national percentages hold true in New Jersey (see Table 2.4). Federal and state funds used for major apprenticeship programs in New Jersey benefit young men almost exclusively. Women however may have received a larger share of the $11.8 million of federal funds for fiscal year 1974 institutional training under the manpower programs (depending on the comparative cost of "women's" and "men's" programs). The $3 million of federal obligations for on-the-job training presumably was heavily weighted toward male trainees.

NEW YORK

Enrollment

In numbers of students and quality of its institutions of higher education, New York is close to the head of the list when state systems of higher education are compared. Under the Master Plan, its prestigious private universities, multibranch State University and City University of New York, together with the extensive scholarship system appear to provide unparalleled opportunities for its young citizens. Yet if we look more closely at the system, we find that young women do not have equal opportunity with young men.

In 1973 girls were just half the total high school graduates but only 46 percent of the full-time degree-credit undergraduate enrollment in New York institutions, and were outnumbered by better than 3:2 in the top-ranking research universities. In public two-year colleges women were only 45 percent. But in the "other four-year" public institutions, which have concentrated on teacher training, women were 51 percent of enrollment.

Women were 44 percent of enrollment in nondegree-credit programs in New York higher education. Of the 9,619 apprenticeships reported to the Equal Employment Opportunity Commission in

1972, 34, or .4 percent, were women. Under the federally funded
manpower training programs women in New York were 41 percent of
those in institutional training.

Funding from Taxes

As indicated above, the older, prestigious private institutions
admit many more young men than young women to undergraduate
status. As national universities these institutions attract promising
young men from all areas of the country, thus leaving fewer places
for resident young women; opportunities for New York women are
likewise less available for enrollment in other states, since women
were outnumbered 3:2 among undergraduate outmigrants. Thus tax
funds appropriated or tax-exemptions given to such research universities provide benefits to young men rather than to young women.

Of the $359 million of federal obligations in fiscal year 1973
for New York higher education, about 60 percent went to private research universities and medical facilities. Likewise, state tax
funds appropriated in the amount of $3.6 million in 1974-75 provided
private medical schools with $1,500 for each full-time student in the
M.D. program, with an additional $6.7 million allotted for medical
and dental schools that increased enrollment. Women in 1972 received 23 percent of all doctorates awarded by New York institutions,
and, among first-professional degrees, 9 percent in medicine and
9 percent in law.

Under the "Bundy" program, since 1968, state funds have been
awarded to private colleges and universities; current funds of $56.9
million in 1974-75 provide $800 for each bachelor's degree awarded,
$600 for each master's degree, and $3,000 for each doctorate. Since
women represented only 42 percent of enrollment in private undergraduate institutions, such use of state funds subsidizes the education
of almost 3 young men for every 2 young women.*

In public institutions also, the State University at Buffalo, with
only 39 percent women, was allotted $67 million from fiscal year
1972 state tax funds while the State College at Buffalo, with 56 percent women, received $18 million. The college has about half the
enrollment of the university at the undergraduate level. The $66
million in federal, state, and local funds expended in fiscal year 1974
for postsecondary vocational education likewise was used to train

---

*Patricia Walsh, "An Analysis of the Participation by Female
Students in the Benefits of the Bundy Program," unpublished study,
Boston University, Department of Economics, June 1975.

TABLE 3.13

Opportunities for Women in Education Beyond High School in New York

	Enrollment in Postsecondary Institutions			Financial Support (in millions of dollars)			
				Tax-Exempt Funds, 1973-74[1]		Tax Funds	
	Women	Total	Women as Percent of Total[g]	Private Business	Private Foundations	State Tax Funds Fiscal Year 1972[2]	Federal Obligations, Fiscal Year 1973[3]
1973 high school graduates[4]	103,353	204,660	50				
I. Academic (degree credit) enrollment							
Fall 1973 full-time undergraduate enrollment, public and private (nonprofit), state total	223,161	484,265	46	n.a.	n.a.	802.3	358.7
A. Research universities, *5 total	16,831	44,266	38	15.1	34.0	67.1	213.5
Public: State University of New York, Buffalo (main campus)[a]	4,633	11,943	39	.3	.2	67.1[d,e]	14.6[f]
Private: Columbia University (main campus)[b]	736	4,344	17	3.2	13.8	n.a.	52.8
Cornell University (main campus)[c]	1,972	6,826	29	2.7	6.5	n.a.	44.1
New York University	2,723	5,927	46	4.3	8.4	n.a.	37.2
University of Rochester	1,772	4,198	42	2.9	2.4	n.a.	26.1
Syracuse University	4,521	9,803	46	.5	.8	n.a.	10.5
Yeshiva University	474	1,225	39	1.2	1.9	n.a.	28.2
B. Excluding research universities							
Public, total	142,200	292,023	49	n.a.	n.a.	n.a.	n.a.
Universities	4,829	9,680	50	n.a.	n.a.	n.a.	n.a.
Other four-year	79,347	154,647	51	n.a.	n.a.	n.a.	n.a.
Two-year	58,024	127,696	45	n.a.	n.a.	131.6	n.a.
Private, total	64,130	147,976	43	n.a.	n.a.	n.a.	n.a.
Universities	16,199	39,544	41	n.a.	n.a.	n.a.	n.a.
Other four-year	43,883	101,778	43	n.a.	n.a.	n.a.	n.a.
Two-year	4,048	6,654	61	n.a.	n.a.	n.a.	n.a.

II. Vocational enrollment

A. Fiscal year 1974 enrollment in state-approved postsecondary, total (unduplicated)[6]	n.a.	74,197	40+[7]
Occupations:			
Trade and industry		12,398	13
Technical		10,849	8
Home economics (gainful)		2,192	84
Health		15,292	92
Office		23,928	62
Distributive		6,361	26
Other		3,177	n.a.
B. Fall 1973 full- and part-time enrollment, public and private (nonprofit; nondegree credit)	8,226	18,707	44
C. Calendar year 1972 apprenticeships, total numbers[9]	34	8,619	.4
D. Fiscal year 1974 MDTA training[10]			
Institutional		6,400	41
JOBS Optional/On-the-Job Training		n.a.	22‡

Federal Obligations, Fiscal Year 1974[11]

29.0
10.5

[a]40 percent women all campuses.
[b]53 percent women all campuses.
[c]36 percent women all campuses.
[d]Additional appropriation: health science centers, $61.7 million; expansion of nursing enrollment, $2.5 million.
[e]Additional $10.4 million for private medical/dental school.
[f]Federal obligations (medical colleges and centers): $39.0 million.
[g]Distribution estimated by Office of Education.

more young men than young women, if percentage distribution follows the national pattern (see Table 2.4).   Federal and state funds
used for major apprenticeship programs in New York benefit young
men almost exclusively. The $29 million of federal obligations in
fiscal year 1974 for institutional training under the manpower programs was used to train almost three young men for every two young
women; the $10 million in on-the-job training funds also benefited
more men, if the national ratio of 4 men to 1 woman holds true in
New York.

OHIO

Enrollment

Women in 1973 were half the graduates of Ohio high schools,
yet in fall 1973 they were just 43 percent of full-time degree-credit
undergraduate enrollment in Ohio, and were outnumbered 3:2 in the
top-ranking research universities. At the public two-year colleges
women were outnumbered almost 2:1.   Of the 20,000 bachelor's degrees received by Ohio women in 1972, 44 percent were in education.

Funding from Taxes

About two-thirds of federal funds obligated in fiscal year 1973
for higher education in Ohio went to the three research universities;
about one-third of state tax fund appropriations likewise went to
these institutions and their related medical facilities. Women in
1972 received 16 percent of doctorates awarded by Ohio institutions,
and, among first-professional degrees, 7 percent in medicine and
5 percent in law. This low percentage of women in medicine, for
example, means that of state tax funds appropriated for education
in medicine and dentistry, only a small fraction will benefit women.
Since the research universities also received almost $13 mil-
lion in corporate gifts and general welfare foundation grants, their
faculty, facilities, and research activities were enhanced. All taxpayers thus involuntarily subsidized the education of about three
young men for every two young women, since these gifts earned
tax-exemptions for their donors; taxes not paid by such donors must
be made up by the rest of the taxpayers.
The $15 million in federal, state, and local funds expended in
fiscal year 1974 for postsecondary vocational education appears to
have been used in like manner to train more young men than young
women, if national percentages hold true for Ohio (see Table 2.4).

Federal and state funds used for major apprenticeship programs
benefited only a handful of young women. The $16 million of fiscal
year 1974 federal funds obligated for institutional and on-the-job
training was used to train about twice as many Ohio men as women.

OKLAHOMA

Enrollment

Women in 1973 were 49 percent of 1973 high school graduates
in Oklahoma but only 41 percent of full-time degree-credit undergraduate enrollment in the state in the fall of 1973. Women were
outnumbered by more than 3:2 in the top-ranking research universities. In public two-year colleges women were a little more than
one-third of enrollment.

Women were 45 percent of enrollment in nondegree-credit
programs of Oklahoma higher education. Of the 780 apprenticeships
reported to the Equal Employment Opportunity Commission in 1972,
one was a woman. Under the federally funded manpower training
programs women in Oklahoma were not much more than one-fifth of
those in institutional training.

Funding from Taxes

About half of the fiscal year 1973 state tax funds appropriated
for operating expenses of higher education went to the research universities and associated medical facilities; about two-thirds of the
fiscal year 1973 federal obligations to Oklahoma higher education
went to these same institutions. Women in 1972 received only 12
percent of doctorates granted by Oklahoma institutions, and, among
first-professional degrees, 7 percent of degrees in medicine and
3 percent in law. Of the 5,300 bachelor's degrees received by
Oklahoma women in 1972, over half were in education.

Since the research universities also received over $1 million
in corporate gifts, and almost as much in foundation grants, their
faculty, facilities, and research activities were enhanced. Since
these gifts earned tax-exemptions for their donors, all taxpayers
thus involuntarily subsidized the education of over 3 young men for
every 2 young women; taxes not paid by such donors must be made
up by the rest of the taxpayers.

The $5 million in federal, state, and local funds expended in
fiscal year 1974 for postsecondary vocational education appears to
have been used to train more young men than young women, if

TABLE 3.14

Opportunities for Women in Education Beyond High School in Ohio

| | Enrollment in Postsecondary Institutions | | | Financial Support (in millions of dollars) | | | |
| | | | | Tax-Exempt Funds, 1973-74[1] | | Tax Funds Fiscal Year 1973 | |
	Women	Total	Women as Percent of Total	Private Business	Private Foundations	State Tax Funds[2]	Federal Obligations[3]
1973 high school graduates[4]	76,146	152,428	50				
I. Academic (degree credit) enrollment							
Fall 1973 full-time undergraduate enrollment, public and private (nonprofit), state total	99,746	229,986	43	n.a.	n.a.	325.1	125.1
A. Research universities,*[5] total	22,205	55,585	40	5.9	6.9	85.1[a]	81.7[b]
Public:							
Ohio State University (main campus)	13,803	33,608	41	2.5	1.8	64.9	44.1
University of Cincinnati (main campus)	7,324	18,705	39	.7	1.2	20.2	15.6
Private:							
Case Western Reserve University	1,078	3,272	33	2.7	3.9	n.a.	22.0
B. Excluding research universities							
Public, total	48,853	109,830	44	n.a.	n.a.	n.a.	n.a.
Universities	37,197	78,937	47	n.a.	n.a.	n.a.	n.a.
Other four-year	9,032	23,655	38	n.a.	n.a.	n.a.	n.a.
Two-year	2,624	7,238	36	n.a.	n.a.	34.7	n.a.
Private, total	28,688	64,571	44	n.a.	n.a.	n.a.	n.a.
Universities	--	--	--	--	--	--	--
Other four-year	28,133	63,526	44	n.a.	n.a.	n.a.	n.a.
Two-year	555	1,045	53	n.a.	n.a.	n.a.	n.a.

II. Vocational enrollment

			Expenditures, fiscal year 1974[8]	
			State/Local 8.4	Federal 6.2
A.	Fiscal year 1974 enrollment in state-approved postsecondary, total (unduplicated)[6]	n.a.	23,002	40†[7]
	Occupations:			
	Trade and industry		1,364	13
	Technical		4,681	8
	Home economics (gainful)		816	84
	Health		7,237	92
	Office		4,056	62
	Distributive		1,731	26
	Other		3,117	n.a.
B.	Fall 1973 full- and part-time enrollment, public and private (nonprofit; nondegree credit)	19,375	43,584	44
C.	Calendar year 1972 apprenticeships, total numbers[9]	16	7,243	.2

			Federal Obligations, Fiscal Year 1974[11]
D.	Fiscal year 1974 MDTA training[10]		
	Institutional	9,800	13.7 36
	JOBS Optional/On-the-Job Training	n.a.	2.7 22‡

[a] Additional appropriations: $9.4 million for University Hospital; $3.0 million for Cincinnati Hospital; $7.9 million for Toledo Medical College and Hospital; $2.7 million for Case Western Reserve Medical and Dental School.

[b] Additional federal obligation: $5.9 million for Toledo Medical College.

TABLE 3.15

Opportunities for Women in Education Beyond High School in Oklahoma

| | Enrollment in Postsecondary Institutions | | | Financial Support (in millions of dollars) | | | |
| | | | | Tax-Exempt Funds, 1973-74[1] | | Tax Funds Fiscal Year 1973 | |
	Women	Total	Women as Percent of Total	Private Business	Private Foundations	State Tax Funds[2]	Federal Obligations[3]
1973 high school graduates[4]	18,320	37,349	49				
I. Academic (degree credit) enrollment							
Fall 1973 full-time undergraduate enrollment, public and private (nonprofit), state total	31,172	76,638	41	n.a.	n.a.	81.7	33.8
A. Research universities,*[5] total	10,420	26,786	39	1.3	.9	31.1	23.3
Public: Oklahoma State University (main campus)	5,493	14,175	39	n.a.	n.a.	15.5	11.2
University of Oklahoma (main campus)	4,927	12,611	39	1.3	.9	15.6[a]	12.1
Private	--	--	--	--	--	--	--
B. Excluding research universities							
Public, total	14,954	37,131	40	n.a.	n.a.	n.a.	n.a.
Universities	466	904	52	n.a.	n.a.	n.a.	n.a.
Other four-year	10,647	25,592	42	n.a.	n.a.	n.a.	n.a.
Two-year	3,841	10,635	36	n.a.	n.a.	4.9	n.a.
Private, total	5,798	12,721	46	n.a.	n.a.	n.a.	n.a.
Universities	1,324	3,331	40	n.a.	n.a.	n.a.	n.a.
Other four-year	3,907	8,006	49	n.a.	n.a.	n.a.	n.a.
Two-year	567	1,384	41	n.a.	n.a.	n.a.	n.a.

Expenditures, fiscal year 1974[8]

	State/Local	Federal
II. Vocational enrollment	13.2	1.4

A. Fiscal year 1974 enrollment in state-approved postsecondary, total (unduplicated)[6]	n.a.	9,899	40+[7]
Occupations:			
Trade and industry	2,207	13	
Technical	3,074	8	
Home economics (gainful)	397	84	
Health	2,116	92	
Office	1,353	62	
Distributive	1,209	26	
Other	n.a.	n.a.	
B. Fall 1973 full- and part-time enrollment, public and private (nonprofit; nondegree credit)	2,438	5,436	45
C. Calendar year 1972 apprenticeships, total numbers[9]	1	780	.1

Federal Obligations
Fiscal Year 1974[11]

D. Fiscal year 1974 MDTA training[10]				
Institutional	2,000	22		4.7
JOBS Optional/On-the-Job Training	n.a.	22‡		.5

a Additional appropriation: Health Sciences Center $10.5 million.

national percentages hold true in Oklahoma (see Table 2.4). Federal and state funds used for major apprenticeship programs in Oklahoma overwhelmingly benefited young men. The $5 million of federal funds obligated in fiscal year 1974 for institutional and on-the-job training presumably were used to train about four young men for every young woman.

PENNSYLVANIA

Enrollment

As Table 3.16 indicates, women in 1973 were 49 percent of high school graduates in 1973 but only 44 percent of full-time degree-credit undergraduate enrollment in the state and were outnumbered by over 3:2 in the top-ranking research universities. Women were 55 percent of enrollment in "other four-year" public institutions which have concentrated on teacher training; of the 23,000 bachelor's degrees received by Pennsylvania women in 1972, 42 percent were in education. At the public two-year colleges women were only 37 percent of enrollment.

Pennsylvania differs from other states in its higher education "system." Penn State University's plant and property is not state owned but private, although the state provides operating expenses; likewise Temple University and the University of Pittsburgh are termed "state-related" and also receive substantial state funding for operating income; only in Pennsylvania is there a tradition of direct and substantial state appropriations to selected private institutions such as the University of Pennsylvania. Taxpayers thus have a direct interest in the enrollment policies of these institutions.

Women were outnumbered by 3:2 in nondegree credit program enrollment in Pennsylvania higher education in 1973. Women were only .1 of those enrolled in the joint union/management apprenticeship programs reported to the Equal Employment Opportunity Commission for fiscal year 1972. Under the federally funded manpower training programs, women in Pennsylvania were only about one-fifth of those in institutional training and presumably equally outnumbered in on-the-job training.

Funding from Taxes

About half of the fiscal year 1972 state tax funds appropriated for operating expenses of higher education went to the research universities and related medical facilities; about 70 percent of federal obligations in fiscal year 1973 to Pennsylvania higher education went to these same institutions. Women in 1972 received 17 percent of the doctorates granted Pennsylvania institutions, and, among first-professional degrees, 17 percent in medicine and 7 percent in law.

Since the research universities also received $8 million in corporate gifts, and $14 million in foundation grants in 1973-74, their faculty, facilities, and research activities were once more enhanced. All taxpayers thus involuntarily subsidized the education of three young men for every two young women, since these gifts earned tax-exemptions for their donors; taxes not paid by such donors must be made up by the rest of the taxpayers.

The $23 million in federal, state, and local funds expended for postsecondary vocational education in fiscal year 1974 also appears to have been used to train about three young men for every two young women, if Pennsylvania follows the national trend (see Table 2.4). Federal and state funds used for apprenticeship programs in Pennsylvania benefited few young women. The $21 million of federal funds obligated in fiscal year 1974 for institutional and on-the-job training were used to train about four young men for every young woman.

SOUTH CAROLINA

Enrollment

Women in 1973 were over half (52 percent) of high school graduates in South Carolina but only 43 percent of full-time degree-credit undergraduate enrollment in the state, and only 38 percent at state universities. At the public two-year colleges women were only one-third of enrollment. Of the almost 4,000 bachelor's degrees received by South Carolina women in 1972, about two-fifths were in education.

Women were one-third of nondegree-credit enrollment in South Carolina higher education in 1973. Of the 285 apprenticeships reported in 1972, just one went to a woman. Under the federally funded manpower training programs women were only about two-fifths of those in institutional training.

Funding from Taxes

The $75 million of state tax funds appropriated in fiscal year 1972 for higher education and the $32 million of federal obligations in

TABLE 3.16

Opportunities for Women in Education Beyond High School in Pennsylvania

| | Enrollment in Postsecondary Institutions | | | Financial Support (in millions of dollars) | | | |
| | | | | Tax-Exempt Funds, 1973-74[1] | | Tax Funds | |
	Women	Total	Women as Percent of Total	Private Business	Private Foundations	State Tax Funds, Fiscal Year 1972[2]	Federal Obligations, Fiscal Year 1973[3]
1973 high school graduates[4]	75,321	154,600	49				
I. Academic (degree credit) enrollment							
Fall 1973 full-time undergraduate enrollment, public and private (nonprofit), state total	109,985	250,751	44	n.a.	n.a.	347.3	184.8
A. Research universities, *[5] total	22,495	57,230	39	8.2	13.8	160.2a	127.9
Public: Penn State University (main campus)	9,006	23,634	38	1.5	.6	74.0	27.8
University of Pittsburgh (main campus)	4,803	11,514	42	1.0	3.0	36.5	29.1
Temple University (main campus)	5,183	11,767	44	.3	.9	39.3	18.3
Private: Carnegie Mellon University	900	2,921	31	1.3	2.2	n.a.	8.2
University of Pennsylvania	2,603	7,394	35	4.1	7.1	10.4	44.5
B. Excluding research universities							
Public, total	45,324	92,387	49	n.a.	n.a.	n.a.	n.a.
Universities	5,930	16,601	36	n.a.	n.a.	n.a.	n.a.
Other four-year	34,155	61,637	55	n.a.	n.a.	n.a.	n.a.
Two-year	5,239	14,149	37	n.a.	n.a.	15.4	n.a.
Private, total	42,166	101,134	42	n.a.	n.a.	n.a.	n.a.
Universities	3,298	10,115	33	n.a.	n.a.	n.a.	n.a.
Other four-year	36,747	87,657	42	n.a.	n.a.	n.a.	n.a.
Two-year	2,121	3,362	63	n.a.	n.a.	n.a.	n.a.

				Expenditures, fiscal year 1974[8]	
				State/Local	Federal
				17.2	6.0

II. Vocational enrollment

A. Fiscal year 1974 enrollment in state-approved postsecondary, total (unduplicated)[6]	n.a.	29,111	40†[7]	
Occupations:				
Trade and industry		4,349	13	
Technical		6,799	8	
Home economics (gainful)		538	84	
Health		8,244	92	
Office		6,533	62	
Distributive		1,192	26	
Other		1,456	n.a.	
B. Fall 1973 full- and part-time enrollment, public and private (nonprofit; nondegree credit)	13,240	33,299	40	
C. Calendar year 1972 apprenticeships, total numbers[9]	81	5,950	.1	
D. Fiscal year 1974 MDTA training[10]				Federal Obligations, Fiscal Year 1974[11]
Institutional		4,100	20	16.6
JOBS Optional/On-the-Job Training		n.a.	22‡	4.5

[a]Additional appropriations for medical facilities: $1.8 million for Penn State; $3.5 million for University of Pittsburgh; $4.6 million for Temple University; $2.6 million for University of Pennsylvania; $5.8 million for other medical institutions.

TABLE 3.17

Opportunities for Women in Education Beyond High School in South Carolina

	Enrollment in Postsecondary Institutions			Financial Support (in millions of dollars)			
				Tax-Exempt Funds, 1973–74[1]		State Tax Funds, Fiscal Year 1972[2]	Federal Obligations, Fiscal Year 1973[3]
	Women	Total	Women as Percent of Total	Private Business	Private Foundations		
1973 high school graduates[4]	18,750	36,150	52				
I. Academic (degree credit) enrollment							
Fall 1973 full-time undergraduate enrollment, public and private (nonprofit), state total	27,496	63,398	43	n.a.	n.a.	75.0	31.7
Public, total	18,113	44,252	41	n.a.	n.a.	n.a.	n.a.
Universities	8,994	23,485	38	n.a.	n.a.	n.a.	n.a.
Other four-year	6,146	11,743	52	1.3	.7	33.0[a]	11.2[b]
Two-year	2,973	9,024	33	n.a.	n.a.	2.4	n.a.
Private, total	9,383	19,146	49	--	--	--	--
Universities	--	--	--	n.a.	n.a.	n.a.	n.a.
Other four-year	8,364	16,470	51	n.a.	n.a.	n.a.	n.a.
Two-year	1,019	2,676	38	n.a.	n.a.	n.a.	n.a.

II. Vocational enrollment

	Women	Total	Women as Percent of Total
A. Fiscal year 1974 enrollment in state-approved postsecondary, total (unduplicated)[6]	n.a.	34,161	40+[7]
Occupations: Trade and industry		6,259	13
Technical		3,953	8
Home economics (gainful)		206	84
Health		2,313	92
Office		5,983	62
Distributive		67	26
Other		15,380[c]	n.a.
B. Fall 1973 full- and part-time enrollment, public and private (nonprofit; nondegree credit)	2,729	8,008	34
C. Calendar year 1972 apprenticeships, total numbers[9]	1	285	.4
D. Fiscal year 1974 MDTA training[10]			
Institutional		800	41
JOBS Optional/On-the-Job Training		n.a.	22‡

Expenditures, fiscal year 1974[8]

State/Local	Federal
25.0	1.1

Federal Obligations, Fiscal Year 1974[11]

	Federal
Institutional	2.4
JOBS Optional/On-the-Job Training	.3

a Additional appropriation: $16.4 million for Medical University of South Carolina.
b Additional federal obligation: $9.2 million for Medical University of South Carolina.
c Includes 288 enrolled in vocational agriculture; rest unidentified.

fiscal year 1973, supported by taxpayers who are parents of girls as well as boys, are being used in a discriminatory fashion. In comparisons among the 20 states of the percentage of women in the professions, South Carolina is lowest: In 1972 women received 2.4 percent of degrees in medicine and less than 1 percent of degrees in law granted by South Carolina institutions.

TEXAS

Enrollment

As Table 3.18 indicates, women in 1973 were about half of high school graduates in Texas but only 43 percent of full-time degree-credit undergraduate enrollment in the state, and only 36 percent of enrollment in the top-ranking research universities. At the public two-year colleges women were outnumbered by more than 3:2. Of the almost 20,000 bachelor's degrees received by Texas women in 1972, almost 40 percent were in education.

Women were a little over one-third of nondegree-credit program enrollment in Texas higher education in 1973. Of the 5,700 apprenticeships reported in Texas in 1972 to the Equal Employment Opportunity Commission, 10 went to women. Under the federally funded manpower training programs, women in Texas in fiscal year 1974 were less than one-fourth of those in institutional and on-the-job training.

Funding from Taxes

About one-third of state tax funds appropriated in fiscal year 1972 for higher education operating expenses went to the research universities and related medical facilities; over half the fiscal year 1973 federal obligations to Texas higher education went to the same institutions. Also, because the University of Texas has a unique advantage of earnings from oil-bearing land granted to it by the legislature in the 1870s (the "available fund"), this institution is able to attract and support top faculty and research activities. Women in 1972 received 17 percent of doctorates granted by Texas institutions, and, among first-professional degrees, 6 percent in medicine and 6 percent in law.

Since the research universities also received $7 million in corporate gifts and $5 million in foundation grants, their faculty, facilities, and research activities were further strengthened. All taxpayers are thus involuntarily subsidizing the education of almost

TABLE 3.18

Opportunities for Women in Education Beyond High School in Texas

| | Enrollment in Postsecondary Institutions | | | Financial Support (in millions of dollars) | | | |
| | | | | Tax-Exempt Funds, 1973-74[1] | | Tax Funds | |
	Women	Total	Women as Percent of Total	Private Business	Private Foundations	State Tax Funds, Fiscal Year 1972[2]	Federal Obligations, Fiscal Year 1973[3]
1973 high school graduates[4]	77,103	153,529	50				
I. Academic (degree credit) enrollment							
Fall 1973 full-time undergraduate enrollment, public and private (nonprofit), state total	121,911	285,032	43	n.a.	n.a.	418.4	190.4
A. Research universities,*[5] total	17,441	47,982	36	7.4	5.4	82.1[a]	50.5[b,c]
Public: University of Texas, Austin	13,804	31,812	43	n.a.	n.a.	54.4	23.1
Texas A & M University	2,981	13,737	22	6.7	3.0	27.7	21.7
Private: Rice University	656	2,433	27	.7	2.4	n.a.	5.7
B. Excluding research universities							
Public, total	82,041	190,359	43	n.a.	n.a.	n.a.	n.a.
Universities	20,965	44,526	47	n.a.	n.a.	n.a.	n.a.
Other four-year	20,294	91,324	44	n.a.	n.a.	47.1	n.a.
Two-year	20,782	54,509	38	n.a.	n.a.	n.a.	n.a.
Private, total	22,429	46,691	48	n.a.	n.a.	n.a.	n.a.
Universities	8,057	15,782	51	n.a.	n.a.	n.a.	n.a.
Other four-year	13,991	29,989	47	n.a.	n.a.	n.a.	n.a.
Two-year	381	920	41	n.a.	n.a.	n.a.	n.a.

Expenditures, fiscal year 1974[8]

	State/Local	Federal
	47.9	5.1

II. Vocational enrollment

A. Fiscal Year 1974 enrollment in state-approved postsecondary, total (unduplicated)[6]	n.a.	72,131	40+[7]
Occupations:			
Trade and industry		22,627	13
Technical		9,530	8
Home economics (gainful)		1,020	84
Health		11,877	92
Office		17,192	62
Distributive		8,596	26
Other		1,289	n.a.
B. Fall 1973 full- and part-time enrollment, public and private (nonprofit; nondegree credit)	15,844	46,522	34
C. Calendar year 1972 apprenticeships, total numbers[9]	10	5,691	.2

			Federal Obligations, Fiscal Year 1974[11]
D. Fiscal year 1974 MDTA training[10]			
Institutional	5,600	24	17.0
JOBS Optional/On-the-Job Training	n.a.	22‡	1.8

[a] Additional appropriations for medical facilities: $63.8 million for University of Texas; $2.1 million for other public institutions; $4.4 million for private institutions; $1.8 million for School of Nursing.

[b] Additional federal obligation: $57.8 million for University of Texas medical centers.

[c] Additional federal obligation: $20.1 million for Baylor Medical School.

twice as many men as women at the research universities, since
these gifts earned tax-exemptions for their donors, which must be
made up by the rest of the taxpayers.

The $53 million of federal, state, and local funds expended in
fiscal year 1974 for postsecondary vocational education in Texas also
appears to have been used to train at least 3 young men for every 2
young women, if 1969 national percentage distribution of enrollment
holds true in Texas (see Table 2.4). Federal and state tax funds
used for major apprenticeship programs in Texas benefited only a
handful of young women. The $19 million of federal funds obligated
in fiscal year 1974 for institutional and on-the-job training apparently
benefited about three times as many men as women.

VERMONT

Enrollment

As Table 3.19 indicates, women were about 51 percent of high
school graduates in Vermont in 1973 and about 49 percent of full-time,
degree-credit undergraduate enrollment in the state. Although Vermont ranks among the smallest of the states in population size, it
has been more equitable in offering educational opportunity to young
citizens of both sexes within the state. However, Vermont in 1968
had the lowest percentage in the nation (67 percent) of undergraduate
students remaining in home state relative to total undergraduate enrollment in higher education anywhere. Men outnumbered women
almost 3:2 among outmigrants. This enrollment pattern makes it
somewhat more difficult to assess the share of educational opportunity available for Vermont women. They are, however, greatly
underrepresented (5 percent) in the public two-year technical colleges.

In vocational training Vermont clearly reversed the national
pattern, with women 76 percent of enrollment in nondegree programs
of higher education in 1973. Likewise, 1974 enrollment under Public
Postsecondary programs is limited to one program in the state, in
the health field, with women estimated at 92 percent of enrollment
(1969 national percentage). Women also predominated in institutional
training under federal manpower programs in fiscal year 1974, with
54 percent of enrollment.

Funding from Taxes

Since Vermont is one of the few states providing assistance to
students at out-of-state colleges, a larger share of the $2.5 million

TABLE 3.19

Opportunities for Women in Education Beyond High School in Vermont

| | Enrollment in Postsecondary Institutions | | | Financial Support (in millions of dollars) | | | |
| | | | | Tax-Exempt Funds, 1973-74[1] | | Tax Funds | |
	Women	Total	Women as Percent of Total	Private Business	Private Foundations	State Tax Funds 1973[2]	Federal Obligations 1973[3]
1973 high school graduates[4]	3,207	6,303	51				
I. Academic (degree credit) enrollment							
Fall 1973 full-time undergraduate enrollment, public and private (nonprofit), state total	9,817	19,935	49	n.a.	n.a.	16.8	12.2
Public, total	4,929	10,024	49	n.a.	n.a.	n.a.	n.a.
Universities	3,493	6,808	51	.2	n.a.	9.5	n.a.
Other four-year	1,409	2,780	51	n.a.	n.a.		n.a.
Two-year	21	436	5	n.a.	n.a.	1.1	n.a.
Private, total	4,888	9,911	49	n.a.	n.a.	n.a.	n.a.
Universities	--	--	--	--	--	--	--
Other four-year	4,214	3,983	47	n.a.	n.a.	n.a.	n.a.
Two-year	674	928	73	n.a.	n.a.	n.a.	n.a.

	Women	Total	Women as Percent of Total
II. Vocational enrollment			
A. Fiscal year 1974 enrollment in state-approved postsecondary, total (unduplicated)[6]	n.a.	262	n.a.
Occupations: Trade and industry		n.a.	n.a.
Technical		n.a.	n.a.
Home economics (gainful)		n.a.	n.a.
Health	262	262	92†
Office		n.a.	n.a.
Distribution		n.a.	n.a.
Other		n.a.	n.a.
B. Fall 1973 full- and part-time enrollment, public and private (nonprofit; nondegree credit)	1,477	1,937	76
C. Calendar Year 1972 apprenticeships, total numbers[9]	0	140	0
D. Fiscal year 1974 MDTA training[10]			
Institutional	200	200	54
JOBS Optional/On-the-Job Training	n.a.	n.a.	22‡

Expenditures, fiscal year 1974[8]

State/Local	Federal
.2	.2

Federal Obligations, Fiscal Year 1974[11]

Federal
.6
.4

funds in scholarship grants presumably goes to young men. However, the $400,000 of federal, state, and local funds for postsecondary vocational training in fiscal year 1974, and the $1 million of federal obligations for manpower training programs, presumably benefited more young women than young men. Whenever tax-derived funds are used arbitrarily to train only one group, whether men or women, taxpayers are being badly served. Academic education and vocational training benefit both the trainee and society. State population, type of industry, and state financial base affect the amount of state funds which can be devoted to those ends, but equitable distribution of tax funds used for education beyond high school is to be desired in Vermont as well as in every other state.

WYOMING

Enrollment

As Table 3.20 indicates, women in 1973 were 49 percent of high school graduates in Wyoming but only 40 percent of full-time, degree-credit undergraduate enrollment in state higher education. Of the 520 bachelor's degrees received by Wyoming women in 1972, about 39 percent were in education.

Women were 40 percent of nondegree-credit program enrollment in Wyoming higher education in 1973, and the same proportion of institutional training under federally funded manpower programs.

Funding from Taxes

The $37 million of state tax funds appropriated for operating expenses of state higher education in fiscal year 1973, and the fiscal year 1974 federal obligations of $6 million, are being used to the benefit of about 3 young men for every 2 young women. Similarly in postsecondary vocational training, the $2 million of federal, state, and local funds expended in fiscal year 1974 were used to train more young men than young women, as was the $1 million in fiscal year 1974 federal obligations for institutional and on-the-job training under manpower programs.

SUMMARY

We have seen that in each state a similar pattern emerges, with but a few exceptions. Women are a minority in the research

TABLE 3.20

Opportunities for Women in Education Beyond High School in Wyoming

| | Enrollment in Postsecondary Institutions | | | Financial Support (in millions of dollars) | | | |
| | | | | Tax-Exempt Funds, 1973-74[1] | | State Tax Funds, Fiscal Year 1973[2] | Federal Obligations, Fiscal Year 1974[3] |
	Women	Total	Women as Percent of Total	Private Business	Private Foundations		
1973 high school graduates[4]	2,781	5,653	49				
I. Academic (degree credit) enrollment							
Fall 1973 full-time undergraduate enrollment, public and private (nonprofit), state total							
Public, total	3,305	8,559	40	n.a.	n.a.	36.6	6.3
Universities	3,305	8,559	40	n.a.	n.a.	n.a.	n.a.
Other four-year	2,469	6,240	40	n.a.	.2	29.9	n.a.
Two-year	--	--	--	--	--	--	--
Private, total	836	2,119	39	n.a.	n.a.	6.7	n.a.
Universities	--	--	--	--	--	--	--
Other four-year	--	--	--	--	--	--	--
Two-year	--	--	--	--	--	--	--

	Women	Total	Women as Percent of Total
II. Vocational enrollment			
A. Fiscal year 1974 enrollment in state-approved postsecondary, total (unduplicated)[6]	n.a.	3,182	40†[7]
Occupations: Trade and industry		1,227	13
Technical		289	8
Home economics (gainful)		0	84
Health		164	92
Office		965	62
Distributive		130	26
Other		407	n.a.
B. Fall 1973 full- and part-time enrollment, public and private (nonprofit; nondegree credit)	845	2,110	40
C. Calendar year 1972 apprenticeships, total numbers[9]	0	277	0
D. Fiscal year MDTA training[10]			
Institutional		300	40
JOBS Optional/On-the-Job Training		n.a.	22‡[11]

Expenditures, fiscal year 1974[8]

State/Local	Federal
1.6	.2

Federal Obligations, Fiscal Year 1974[11]

Federal
.8
.2

universities and in public two-year degree-credit programs; they
are often a majority in the "other four-year" public institutions
specializing in teacher training. In vocational training also, to the
extent that sex distribution in most states follows the national pattern (see Table 2.4), women remain a minority in the programs
leading to employment at high-skilled trades and a majority in training for the low-skilled, "blocked lower ranks" of paraprofessionals.
Parents of girls as well as boys, through their taxes, pay for this
system that provides different and inferior opportunities for lifetime careers for women.

Decisions on curriculum, admissions, and guidance are made
by education professionals, rather than by the tax-paying public.
The discriminatory selection of young men to be trained as future
scholars, doctors, lawyers, government officials, or as welders,
machinists, engineers is being made by the leaders of education.
In the next chapter we will look at the possible economic motivation
inducing these leaders to make discriminatory choices with respect
to admission of students to career preparatory studies.

4

ECONOMIC MOTIVATION FOR DISCRIMINATION AGAINST WOMEN IN EDUCATION

Richard Lester of Princeton University is among the latest to view with alarm the possibility that women are seeking equality with men in employment in higher education. One hundred years ago President Lowell of Harvard wondered whether higher education for women was not a disservice to society. Lester particularly fears the effects of an invasion by women faculty of the "major" universities. He defines the "major" universities as those "three or four dozen" most outstanding in the country "in terms of advanced education and research in the arts and sciences" ranking in the top level by such measures as assessments of graduate education by the American Council on Education (ACE); number of Ph. D. s granted per year; volume of research contribution to scholarly publication; dollar volume of research; awards to faculty (Nobel Prize, and so forth), pointing out: "They are in strong competition with one another for financial and other community support, for the best . . . students . . . and the best faculty in different subject areas." Can there be discrimination in student admissions in such a competitive situation?[1]

Economist Gary Becker was among the first to express discrimination in economic terms, proposing that we recognize that individuals may have a "taste for discrimination"; the individual must either pay or forfeit income to indulge this taste. This applies to employers, workers, and customers: Employers would be willing to pay higher wages because their "taste for discrimination" restricts the labor supply to a favored group; workers would be willing to take lower wages rather than work beside persons of other races; customers would be willing to pay higher prices rather than purchase goods produced or sold by persons of other races (or other creeds, colors, sex, and so on).[2]

Although Becker recognizes that white workers actually may temporarily gain advantage (in the division of a given output) from the exclusion of blacks in job competition, he relies on long-run competitive market forces to eliminate such discrimination. Eventually, the entry of a competing employer who will, for example, hire blacks (and thus incur lower wage costs) will force the discriminating employer to integrate his work force or leave the industry.

But suppose that in the case of higher education Becker's model does not apply. That is, suppose that an individual who has a "taste for discrimination" is given a reward, and further that the reward varies directly with the magnitude of his taste for discrimination. In such a case we cannot rely on competitive market forces to end discrimination, but rather must expect that increasing economic leverage will accrue to those who discriminate, thus that discriminatory practices will be reinforced. Is this model relevant to education beyond high school? Let us look in turn at postsecondary academic and vocational education to see whether penalties or rewards are operative upon discriminatory behavior in these areas.

ACADEMIC EDUCATION

As in most other areas, from professional sports to the choirs of angels, there is a hierarchy among the roughly 2,500 institutions of higher education classified by the U.S. Office of Education. Perhaps 50 to 100 of these institutions with group composition varying somewhat over time may be considered top-ranked universities and technical institutes; below these come top liberal arts colleges and less-prestigious universities, then lesser liberal arts colleges and teachers' colleges; the two-year colleges; and finally "finishing schools" or former business schools or other schools that may be only recently collegiate.

Quality

To classify institutions as to "overall quality" is a risky business, especially at the undergraduate level, although there have been a few attempts to do so. Several major elements enter into such as assessment and perhaps may include "quality" of faculty (measured by percent with doctorate); selectivity (measured by median SATs of entering undergraduates); library and laboratory resources per student, and similar characteristics. The Carnegie Commission defines "research universities" in terms that reflect such institutional quality: those institutions among the 100 institutions leading in federal financial support over a period of years, who awarded at least 50 Ph. Ds (or M. D. s) in 1969-70.[3] The Carnegie Commission further classifies higher education into comprehensive universities, liberal arts colleges, two-year colleges, and specialized institutions (theology, schools of art, music, and the like).

This ranking does not imply that there are not some brilliant and inspiring faculty at two-year colleges, as well as some mediocre or at least incomprehensible faculty at high-ranked universities. Nevertheless, a brilliant teacher will be limited by the inadequate library and laboratory facilities of the smaller schools, while the inadequate teacher in a university may be of smaller consequence because of the associated highly qualified faculty and student body, as well as the depth of library and laboratory facilities. As we noted in Chapter 2, the top-ranked research universities admit fewer women than men to their undergraduate colleges. Is there a penalty or reward to these institutions for their discriminatory policies?

As economist Allan Cartter once noted, academic economists have not to any great extent studied their own institutions. As another economist, Everett Burtt, has noted: "Value judgments affect economists' decisions as to which problems they will analyze; they influence the choice of variables to be included; and they affect the grounds on which the results of the investigations are judged."[4] The present study explicitly professes the value of equal educational opportunity for the equally qualified, regardless of sex (or any other characteristic), in the interests of the greater welfare of society, as well as the greater satisfaction of the individual. In that light, let us look at the possible economic motivations of the decision makers, faculty as well as administration, in higher education.

The product and labor markets in which these institutions operate are difficult to classify. There is an unusual interdependency between product and labor market, such that the "products" (the graduating students) may return to compete in the "labor market" with the faculty who produced them. The institutions are nonprofit and yet necessarily interested in economic survival. Who is "investing" in this production process, and why?

Investment in "Human Capital"--
Who Makes the Decision?

For some years now there has been considerable interest in the "human capital" approach to education. It has been suggested that the constantly improving level of education of the American labor force has been mainly responsible for the growth in national output over the past 70 years. It can be demonstrated that, on the average, the individual's lifetime earnings vary with the years of school completed. Thus it is argued that it is in the interest of society to "invest" in the education of its youth, and for an individual to "invest" in his own education, thereby increasing human capital. But we must ask further: To what extent does the investment decision rest with either society or the individual, and to what extent does this decision rest with the educational institutions themselves?

Society (through government) can grant scholarships or other financial aid but cannot determine that an individual shall attend a particular institution; the individual can determine neither his acceptance by a particular institution nor, in most cases, his ability to finance attendance if accepted. Only the particular institution can make both these decisions. Thus if there is a firm basis for the concept of human capital, it rests on the decisions of the educational institution to invest or not to invest in a particular 18-year old.

As with any other investment decision, certain criteria are applied: Are there alternative investments that would have a greater payoff? What is the relative risk involved? What is the relevant time frame? Is the investment expected to pay off immediately, or in the long run? That the university considers these questions in a "nonprofit" context does not alter the importance of these questions and answers. For mere economic survival, the university must look to its "market" for revenue as well as to its costs. Becker suggested that the typical investor in human capital is "more impetuous" than his counterpart investing in physical capital, but his analysis was not directed to the situation of the cautious educational administrator, weighing the "returns" from investing in Applicant M rather than Applicant W, both seeking undergraduate admission.

It has long been accepted that the tuition paid by students does not cover the costs of their education at top-level universities, although Cartter suggests that this may be true only for graduate students. At any rate, other sources must be found to assume the costs of educating the next generation of humanists, scientists, and political leaders. Basically (excluding tuition and fees) there are three main sources of funds for this purpose: income from endowments of past donors; current gifts and grants from private donors; and government subsidies including scholarships, fellowships, or research contracts. Since income from past endowments very often lags behind the fast-rising university costs, it is necessary for the major institutions to attract a share of the funds currently dispensed by private donors and foundations, and by state and federal governments.

In obtaining funding from corporate or foundation sources, reputation is of the "utmost importance." Similarly, as the Orlans study reported,[5] the allocation of federal research funds is highly correlated with faculty recognition and scholarly achievement, although any political leverage would be an added advantage in the latter case. Such reputation derives not only from faculty theoretical break-throughs or major empirical studies, but from the quality of students produced by the faculty, as these graduates are perceived by other institutions or government review boards.

Thus, although student tuition represents a substantial source of income, the major university market does not deal with the student principally as "customer." The student might better be conceived of as a private donor usually of limited means, contributing what he can afford, and is "assessed" to support the university he attends. The main transaction is the "sale" of university expertise to interested donors, foundations, and government at all levels in developing the pool of talent within each year's high school graduates. Like a technical consultant to an oil company (or a dowser to a household) the university points out to individual donors, private foundations, and various governments the likely sources of new talent. The university further can provide the technical skills to pump out or otherwise extract the valuable energy, skills, and insights stored in the individual freshman. (Some might wish to add that the university can also assist in preserving the status quo, from a class viewpoint, by admitting mainly upper-income youth. However, that is a different question, well treated by Samuel Bowles, Michael Reich, and others.[6] In view of the universal financial problems of higher education, such preferential admissions can be viewed here as simply another method whereby the university seeks to conserve its scarce resources by seeking a number of affluent parents for tuition now and donations later.)

Before abandoning this analogy of the student as national resource (because it becomes difficult to maintain), we should nevertheless emphasize its relevance. The bright potential humanists, scientists, political leaders, and scholars must be given every opportunity to develop their talents for the sake of society as well as their own future. The leading U.S. colleges and universities, public and private, have produced Nobel laureates in many fields, have advanced national welfare, improved individual health, made possible commercial developments. But they have not admitted women on an equal basis with men. In the context of intelligent decision making, in the competitive drive for the "best students," the "best faculty," why have the universities been so reluctant to include women?

If we begin in the context of "things as they are," we recognize the basis for the university's decision. Society does not value women as indicated by the examples in Chapter 2, and in many more instances that could be cited. The leadership of society--in the church, courts, military, medicine, government--is male. It is the conventional wisdom that investment in the education of bright women will have a lower payoff than an equal investment in an equally bright man because of society's reluctance to accept, or pay for, work attributed to women. Without absolving the university of its share of responsibility for perpetuating this view of women, let us explore the basis of that evaluation.

Performance and Perception Ratings

One of the many attractions of sports lies in the simplicity of its "performance rating." One need not be an expert to enjoy and appreciate a good shot, or pass, or drive. The best golfer emerges as the player who plays a round in the least number of strokes; the best basketball player as the one who drops the most baskets; the best baseball player as the one who produces the most runs; and so on. Although officials are called on for decisions in disputed areas, the fundamental principles of most sports are obvious even to a layman. Either the ball passes through the hoop or it does not. No subjective decision is needed in performance rating.

It is otherwise in the academic world, where much of the scholarly production is incomprehensible to a layman. In each discipline, specialists pass on the achievements of their peers in what has been described as "perception rating." If an article or book or experiment is perceived by fellow scientists or humanists as a theoretical breakthrough, or a fundamental restructuring of the field, there will be a competitive scramble by the major universities to lure the scholar away from his present campus. Under such a perception rating system, female scholars, whether students or faculty, generally rank lower simply because they are female. It is equally true in professional societies that women lawyers are rarely perceived as potential judges, nor women doctors as chiefs of hospital divisions.

Thus in attempting to maximize the value of its "output," each individual university is highly rational in its policy of discriminatory admissions. To paraphrase a prominent male chauvinist of an earlier era, it is likely that no university president assumes office intent on depreciating his institution. The faculty likewise have a keen interest in the economic viability of the institution. Recalling that the main sources of university funds--from government agencies, private foundations, and private individual and corporate donors-- represent grants to the institutions perceived to be most productive, it is obvious that a move toward equal admissions by a single university would be counterproductive.

The university's output is represented by each year's graduating seniors, as well as its crop of Ph.Ds, M.D.s, and so on.

The "quality" of this output is judged in terms of perception rating by other universities seeking graduate students and faculty, by government agencies awarding research contracts, by private donors and foundations seeking to advance knowledge. Income from past endowment grows ever smaller as a percent of current expenditures, but new donors, new federal research contracts, and new foundation grants depend on an institution's reputation. That reputation must suffer should it become apparent that a university is wasting its resources developing the talents of young women who will not be accepted and employed by society as physicists, lawyers, business executives, bankers, judges, doctors, senators, presidents. Although for that reason the woman alumna will be less able to remember her Alma Mater in lifetime gifts or final bequests, such a long-run consideration pales to insignificance when placed beside the possibility of grant curtailment or gift shrinkage as it directly affects the salary and other rewards of current faculty and administration. The strong resistance by top private universities to entering what was perceived as the very "chancy" field of educating women found expression in vigorous and successful lobbying for the Erlenborn Amendment, [7] by which private undergraduate education was exempted from the equal admissions requirements of Title IX. Since these top private institutions guarding the gates of undergraduate admissions against equal numbers of women are at the same time effectively denying the excluded women equal opportunity for graduate and professional study and careers, such discrimination is highly costly over the long term to women. Analysis of the economic motivation of faculty and administrators of these institutions can provide a rationale, if not a justification, of such policies.

The questions arising out of equal admissions policies directly affect the economic welfare of the current faculty and administration. Will the young women baccalaureates be accepted for graduate and professional studies at other universities? Will they be hired by other "major" institutions, advance to professorial status, and begin to send back a stream of promising applicants for the graduate departments? Will these young women be perceived as making important scholarly contributions, which will be published in the major journals, thus maintaining the reputation of the baccalaureate institution? Will the young woman student be perceived by site committees deciding on research grants as a worthy research partner? To every question, the response is in terms of perception rating rather than performance rating. If the perception of male decision makers (awarding grants and gifts) is unfavorable, then the relative standing of the equal-admissions institution will decline, with adverse effects on further grants, contracts, and gifts. If such sources of funds dry up, the university and college faculty and administrators, as well as library and other facilities, must suffer.

Which university decision maker would support equal admissions of the sexes, faced with such a prospect? Despite differences in other areas, faculty and administration can only be united in their determination to maintain their relative standing among fellow institutions. In John Dunlop's terms, slipping out of the "major university wage contour"[8] into the "comprehensive university wage contour" may mean not only lower direct rewards (faculty salary), but less research funding, fewer bright students to work with (both male and female), fewer "visible" faculty colleagues as partners on research proposals, thus less opportunity to build one's own name and reputation (and salary and fees) through publications in the journals, appointment to review and advisory boards. To an economist the decision of faculty and administration at any major or would-be major institution of higher education to maintain a low "femininity" index (to use Howard Bowen's terminology with respect to industry)[9] is highly rational.

But, although each individual university makes an economically rational decision to refrain from equal admissions policies, the sum of those decisions leads to a perpetuation of the problem. Because women have low perception ratings, institutions with a high representation of women undergraduates are less likely to impress those within government agencies, private foundations, or private philanthropists who have funds to distribute. Such institutions, with smaller funds, cannot pay salaries to attract top faculty, add to library holdings, build new laboratories, offer financial aid to students. Thus the institution becomes less attractive to the brightest graduate and undergraduate students. As a result, the output of the university decreases in perceived value, and the institution's ability to attract new funds diminishes even further. The decision of other institutions to keep a "favorable" (predominantly male) sex ratio of undergraduates is thus reinforced, and, coincidentally, the question of sex discrimination in graduate and professional school admissions has been covertly solved. A good many of the brightest young women, from low- or moderate-income families are out of the contest to become lawyers, doctors, or scholars because they have not been admitted as undergraduates to top-ranking universities and given financial aid that would have been available to similarly qualified young men.

However economically rational the basis for sex-discriminatory admissions, such a decision by institutions receiving public funds is unacceptable, in the light of the new consciousness of American women. The mother who realizes in middle age that her own options for education were foreclosed does not wish her daughter to go down that same road. If the present economic payoffs to sex-discriminatory undergraduate enrollment in major universities discourage the adoption of effective equal-admissions policies, there is only one answer:

Let us change the payoffs. This method will also prove effective in changing the analogous situation with respect to opportunities for vocational training for women, to which we now turn.

VOCATIONAL EDUCATION

The Coleman study entitled Equality of Educational Opportunity includes a questionnaire designed for sixth-grade children. The following question is asked in the form shown below:[10]

53. When you finish school, what sort of job do you think you will have? Pick the one that is the closest.

Boys answer from the selections below

(a) Draftsman or medical technician
(b) Banker, company officer, or government official
(c) Store owner or manager, office manager
(d) Sales clerk, office clerk, truck driver, waiter, policeman, bookkeeper, mailman, barber
(e) Salesman
(f) Farm or ranch manager or owner
(g) Farm worker on one or more than one farm
(h) Factory worker, laborer, or gas station attendant
(i) Doctor, lawyer, clergyman, engineer, scientist, teacher, professor, artist, accountant
(j) Carpenter, electrician, mechanic, tailor, or foreman in a factory
(k) Don't know

Girls answer from the selections below

(a) Housewife only
(b) Doctor, lawyer, scientist
(c) Beautician
(d) Bookkeeper or secretary
(e) Waitress or laundry worker
(f) School teacher
(g) Nurse
(h) Saleslady
(i) Maid or domestic servant
(j) Factory worker
(k) Don't know

Without commenting on the inclusion of such a question in a volume so entitled let us turn to our main concern.

How can we explain the persistence of sex stereotyping in occupational training? Can we apply the same economic rationale that

explains the reluctance of male faculty and administrators to admit
women to the learned professions? Does it fit the case of vocational
administration and faculty?

It is the elementary public schools that have taught girls at an
early age that carpentry and electrical circuits are reserved for boys.
But it is the vocational education faculty in "trades and industry" and
"technical" instruction that has a direct economic interest in maintaining high male enrollments.

Job Descriptions and Sex-Stereotyping
in the Skilled Trades

Resistance to the entry of women into the skilled trades takes
two forms: (1) a denial that an occupation associated with women
has a high skill content; and (2) a refusal to train women for "male"
jobs already classified as skilled. The Wisconsin Apprentice Study
by Patricia Mapp calls attention to the 3-digit code used in the Dictionary of Occupational Titles to indicate the degree of complexity
in dealing with three areas: data, people, things. Ratings in each
of the three areas range from 0 (very complex) to 8 (demanding very
little skill (see Appendix F). A nursery school teacher is classified
in the Dictionary as an 878 rating (the same accorded a parking lot
attendant), slightly lower in skill than a "pet shop attendant" (877)--
far lower than the dog-trainer (228).[11] This is not just an exercise
in classification; a low-skilled job will not be recognized as "apprenticeable." On that classification hinges the possibility of federal
funds to unions, their male officers, the male graduates of the apprentice system who become classroom instructors, the male community college and postsecondary vocational and industrial arts faculty, whose pay and promotion opportunities are enhanced by funded
demand for training apprentices and workers in the skilled trades.

Earnings Patterns

Tables 1.3 and 1.4 (see Chapter 1, pp. 14-21) demonstrate the earnings pattern of men and women, a pattern famil-
iar to faculty and administrators of shop and vocational programs:
The higher paid occupations are predominantly male. The adverse
effects of a shift (toward more females) in the sexual composition of
an occupation would directly and adversely affect the economic interest of the faculty and administration in that field. In the Monthly
Labor Review article accompanying Table 1.3 it was pointed
out that "the chances of an occupation falling in a high earnings decile

for men are greatly decreased as the proportion of female workers increases. . . . Men in occupations dominated by women, while earning more than the women, are likely to earn less than men in other occupations."[12]

This is borne out by Table 1.3, which shows railroad conductors and engineers leading the blue-collar group in annual earnings (with women 1 percent of employment). The low percentage of women among photoengravers and lithographers (women 13 percent), tool and die makers (women 2 percent), pattern makers (5 percent), computer repair (2 percent), foreman (not elsewhere classified) (8 percent), millwrights (1 percent), electroplaters (5 percent), power station operators (4 percent)--all in the top 20 percent of male occupations ranked by 1969 earnings--confirms this relationship.

In the top 20 percent of occupations ranked by 1969 median male earnings, only one occupation (and that one footnoted as a statistical fluke) had more than 50 percent of women in the occupation; most had a very small percentage of women. By contrast, in the bottom 20 percent of occupations ranked by male earnings, over half the occupations had more than 50 percent women in the occupation (see Table 1.4).

The implications are clear--it doesn't pay to be associated with women. In fact, in the blue-collar fields, if a woman can do it, it raises doubts as to whether it is in fact an "apprenticeable" skill as defined by the Department of Labor and therefore may not require "related instruction" that provides funding to the technical and trades faculty.

Under the circumstances it is not surprising that educators and administrators in these fields should resist the entrance of women into these programs. The close association between the prestige (income) of an occupation and the prestige (income) of a teacher in that field (within the same wage contour) provides the economic incentive for reluctance to teach women the trade secrets.

Given the prevailing view of the capability of women, vocational administrators and faculty have reason to fear that the cornucopia of funds created by the 1963 and 1968 federal vocational legislation might be diminished if training is "wasted" on women. The unwillingness to permit the skilled trades to lose ground in earnings rank requires that funds allotted for the education of girls and women be used in a narrow band of low-skilled occupations. Fortuitously this leaves a larger proportion of funds at the disposition of male faculty and administrators in trades and industry fields, for salaries as well as equipment, and keeps the industrial arts faculty within the high-wage contour.

We can identify then in the area of vocational education an economic motivation behind the resistance of unions and vocational

faculty to the admission of women to skilled trades and industrial
training. We have likewise indicated that the possibility of a decline
in prestige (income) of faculty and administration lies behind the resistance to admitting women as students (and a fortiori faculty).

SUMMARY

We must recognize that there is a circularity here. Unions
and educators, academic as well as vocational, correctly perceive
that women and their work are not valued by society. A recent study
asked two groups of male and female students to rate the prestige of
five high-status professions (architect, professor, lawyer, physi-
cian, scientist). The experimental group was given a prediction that
women would comprise a majority in the given field in the next 25
years, while the control group was informed that no change in the
proportion of women was expected. Findings were that ratings of
occupational prestige and desirability decreased when subjects an-
ticipated increased proportions of women in the profession (in four
cases, at .05 or better significance levels).[13] It is asking too much
of any one university (or vocational school or union) that it should
decide unilaterally to admit women on an equal basis. Such a course
of action would appear, and may be, a threat to the economic prosperity (and relative prestige ranking) of the particular college, university, vocational school, or union, and thus likely to be resisted
by decision-making officers, administrators, and faculty.

Some method then must be found to assist these institutions to
move toward equality for women without incurring intolerable economic penalties. Such methods are suggested in Chapter 5.

NOTES

1. Richard Lester, Antibias Regulation of Universities:
Faculty Problems and Their Solutions (New York: McGraw-Hill,
1974), pp. 7, 8.

2. Gary Becker, "Economics of Discrimination," in Labor
Economics and Labor Relations, ed. L. Reynolds and Moser Masters
(Englewood Cliffs, N.J.: Prentice-Hall, 1974), pp. 181-85.

3. Carnegie Commission on Higher Education, A Classification of Institutions of Higher Education (Berkeley, Calif., 1973),
pp. 2-3.

4. Everett J. Burtt, Social Perspectives in the History of
Economic Theory (New York: St. Martin's Press, 1972), p. 4.

5. H. Orlans, "The Effects of Federal Programs on Higher Education," in A Statistical Portrait of Higher Education, ed. S. Harris (New York: McGraw-Hill, 1972), p. 399.

6. Samuel Bowles, Schooling and Inequality from Generation to Generation (Cambridge, Mass.: Center for Education Policy Research, 1971). Report No. 8; Michael Reich, "The Economics of Racism," in Reynolds and Masters, op. cit., pp. 186-91.

7. U.S. Congress, House, Congressional Record, H-10365, November 4, 1971 (see Appendix G).

8. John T. Dunlop, "The Task of Contemporary Wage Theory," in The Theory of Wage Determination, ed. John T. Dunlop (New York: St. Martin's Press, 1957), pp. 16-20.

9. Howard Bowen, Economics of Labor Force Participation (Princeton, N.J.: Princeton University Press, 1969).

10. U.S. Department of Health, Education, and Welfare, Equality of Educational Opportunity (Coleman Report) (Washington, D.C., 1966), p. 632.

11. Patricia Mapp, Women in Apprenticeship--Why Not? U.S. Department of Labor, Manpower Research Monograph No. 33 (Washington, D.C., 1974), pp. 17-20.

12. Dixie Sommers, "Occupational Rankings for Men and Women by Earnings," Monthly Labor Review, U.S. Department of Labor, August 1974, p. 50.

13. John C. Touhey, "Effects of Additional Women Professionals on Ratings of Occupational Prestige and Desirability," Journal of Personality and Social Psychology 29, no. 1 (1974): 86-89.

CHAPTER

5

SUGGESTIONS FOR ACHIEVING
EQUAL EDUCATIONAL
OPPORTUNITY

Alden Thresher, former admissions director of the Massachusetts Institute of Technology, put it well: "As the saying goes, the doctor can bury his mistakes. The university has been able to render its mistakes invisible by condemning them to non-education and hence, for the most part, to non-performance--a perfect example of the self-fulfilling prophecy."[1] American women have been denied equal admission to top-ranked undergraduate education, and thus to equal representation among leaders in science, scholarship, and government.

The same charge can be made with reference to American vocational education, which has denied women access to training in basic math and machine skills, thereby perpetuating the stereotype of the incompetent woman. In a society in which economic survival rests on the twin pillars of money and machinery, women have been educated to believe they cannot hammer a nail or balance a checkbook.

For most low- and moderate-income families, financing the four years of undergraduate education represents a considerable burden. On this topic, a spokesman for the American Council on Education commented before a Congressional committee:

> During the course of my study . . . a number of
> things struck me with particular force. One was
> the . . . anomaly in which we as a nation provide
> free education for all through Grade 12, and for
> most who are capable of it after grade 16; while
> at the same time we mark off four years as a
> sink-or-swim period and let those who are strong
> enough to do it on their own resources attempt the
> passage [emphasis added].[2]

As the present study shows, it is mostly young women who are thus left to sink or swim through the undergraduate years--who are denied equal admission to the top universities that control most financial aid--and, not surprisingly, a good many young women sink. To complete the exclusion of women from leading professions, spokesmen for the major universities can then "discover" that there are fewer "qualified" young women applicants for graduate school, law, or medical school, since they have attended low-rated undergraduate institutions. Thus the many pious declarations that "equal admissions" policies are being followed in graduate and professional schools: "If there is a discrepancy, then it's God's doing and society's doing, not ours."[3] As Oregon Representative Edith Green pointed out, equal graduate admissions guaranteed by Title IX (see Appendix A) are meaningless,[4] unless women are admitted in equal numbers, and given equal financial aid, across the spectrum of undergraduate college types. Since women now are not represented in equal numbers as undergraduates in the leading universities that are the "proving ground" for advanced work, they cannot present "equal qualifications" to graduate institutions.

In the area of skill training also, fewer young women are admitted to vocational schools and programs funded by state and federal monies, or given as many opportunities to "learn while earning" as apprentices. Because women are only a minority of those admitted to publicly financed programs, they must struggle to provide themselves with skills through private (for-profit) vocational schools, which are not always carefully monitored by state education agencies. Because of their inability to judge the claims made by these schools, some young women, like the 19-year old quoted in the Boston Globe "Spotlight" series, who "ran down and took out all my savings," may be paying for worthless courses, while their brothers receive excellent training in publicly financed programs.

PROGRESS FOR WOMEN IN EDUCATION SINCE 1900

In view of recent legislation with respect to equal educational opportunity, at both state and federal levels, it may appear to the casual observer that the situation noted above is rapidly changing and that no further action is required. Women, it seems, are now moving in greater numbers through "equal-access" programs, into top colleges and universities that offer the most financial aid to undergraduates, the most highly qualified faculty, the best facilities of library and laboratory, the greatest opportunity for selection as Wilson fellows and similar awards leading to enhanced opportunities for satisfying careers. It appears that women are being encouraged by "affirmative action" programs to enter apprenticeships and other skilled training.

Many of the major universities--Yale, Berkeley, Stanford-- have in the past few years increased the numbers of women admitted to undergraduate status (some having started at "zero"). Harvard has recently been considering a plan for equal access that considers applicants on their "merits," rather than limiting admissions of women to a fixed percent (29 percent) as at present. The U.S. Department of Labor has established an "Apprenticeship Outreach" program for women, similar to that already established for minorities. Admissions of more women are reported at law and medical schools across the country. Can we then assume that from now on women will be represented at all education levels, and in all occupations, in proportion to their numbers in the population?

If history has any lessons, such an outcome is doubtful unless women take action to ensure it. In 1927, in the bright aftermath of the women's suffrage movement, the number of women Ph. D. candidates inspired the comment, "it augurs well for the future." However, the percentage of women among peacetime recipients of the Ph. D. reached a peak in the early 1930s that was not attained again until 1972 (see Figure 5.1). Likewise, the wartime rise in women workers in the skilled trades was checked in the 1940s by the return of male veterans. According to Edie Van Horn, former chief steward in the United Automobile Workers, "After the war all the work ground to a halt. All of a sudden women were getting lower pay than before. Companies were keeping separate seniority lists for men and women. During the war women were doing the jobs that men did. . . . Does it take a war to achieve equal rights?"[5] Women in the 1970s represent less than 1 percent of apprenticeships and less than 10 percent of workers in most skilled trades.

The popular press understandably emphasizes the "news" of breakthroughs for an occasional woman in admission to law or medical school, or to colleges formerly all male, or to "men's jobs." But if we look at the evidence, that is, the trend in the representation of women in academic or vocational programs, it would seem premature to celebrate. Figures 5.1, 5.2, 5.3, and 5.4 indicate that "progress" in these areas has been slow at best and women in 1975 may actually represent a smaller percent of degree recipients, or of vocational trainees, than was true earlier. For example:

1. Bachelor's Degrees: The latest full report by the U.S. Office of Education on degrees conferred indicates that women in 1972 received 43.7 percent of all bachelor's degrees, a substantial rise above the low point of less than 25 percent during the 1950s. But in 1940, the previous peak (excluding war years), women received 41.3 percent of total "bachelor's and first-professional" degrees

FIGURE 5.1

Women as a Percentage of Bachelor's* and First-Professional Degrees, Selected Years, 1900-72

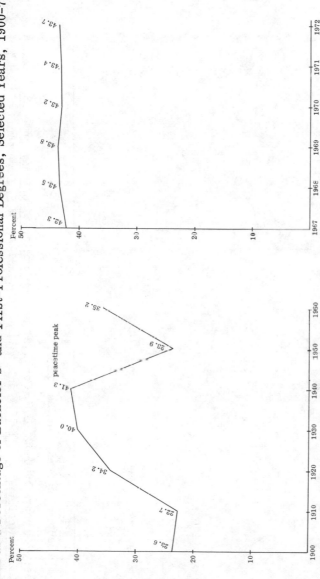

*Prior to 1961, all first level degrees (bachelor's and first-professional) were reported as combined figures. Thus, the percentages shown understate the percentage of women among bachelor's degree recipients.

Note: Percentages computed by the author.

Sources: For years 1900-57: U.S. Census Bureau, Historical Statistics of U.S., series H-327-338; 1960: idem, Statistical Abstract, 1975, Table 237, p. 141; 1967-72: U.S. Department of Health, Education, and Welfare, Earned Degrees Conferred, 1972, Table 1, p. 7.

135

FIGURE 5.2

Women as a Percentage of Doctorates, Selected Years, 1900–72

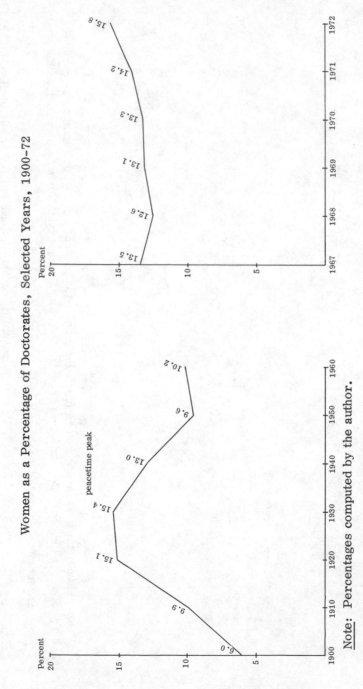

Note: Percentages computed by the author.

Sources: For years 1900–50: U.S. Census Bureau, Historical Statistics of the U.S., series H–327–338; 1960: idem, Statistical Abstract, 1975, Table 237, p. 141; 1967–72: U.S. Department of Health, Education, and Welfare, Earned Degrees Conferred, 1972, Table 1, p. 7.

136

FIGURE 5.3

Women as a Percentage of Degrees in Medicine, 1950–72, and in Law, Selected Years, 1955–72

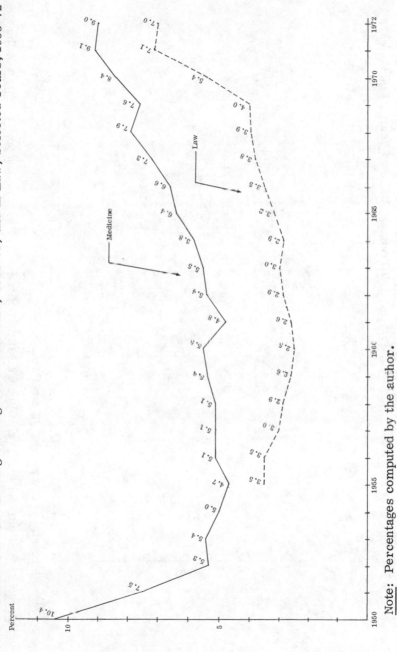

Note: Percentages computed by the author.

Sources: For years 1950–71: U.S. Department of Health, Education, and Welfare, Education Digest 1974, Table 114, p. 101, note 1; 1972: idem, Earned Degrees Conferred, 1972, Table 9, pp. 734–35.

FIGURE 5.4

Women as a Percentage of MDTA Institutional and On-the-job Training, Selected Years, Fiscal Years 1963-74

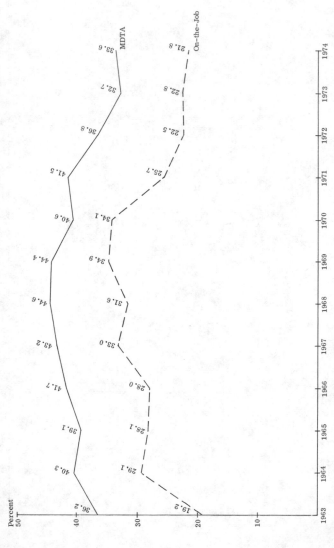

Note: Percentages computed by the author.

Sources: Institutional training, all years: U.S. Department of Labor, Manpower Report of the President, 1975, Table F-4, p. 321; on-the-job training, 1963-70: idem, Manpower Report of the President, 1971, Table F-7; 1971: idem, Manpower Report of the President, 1972, Table F-8; 1972: idem, Manpower Report of the President, 1973, Table F-8; 1973, idem, Manpower Report of the President, 1974, Table F-10; 1974: idem, Manpower Report of the President, 1975, Table F-9.

(the two were published as one figure until the 1960s). Even using
this artificially low figure (the bachelor's degree percentage in 1940
must be higher, since women have never been well represented in
first-professional degrees), it appears that it has taken more than
30 years for women to increase their share of bachelor's degrees by
two percentage points; a corrected figure, adjusted by removing the
professional degree recipients, would show almost no change since
1940.

Women's percentage of enrollment in higher education, which
has been rising in recent years, may in fact have reached a plateau.
This study has used 1973 enrollment figures (this is the latest complete tabulation published). However, preliminary enrollment figures
for 1974 and 1975 have been released by the U.S. Office of Education. [6] These figures do not show a breakdown by level (undergraduate, graduate, etc.) and therefore cannot be compared directly with
the 1973 data shown in Table 1.1. Nevertheless, these figures show
women as 42.8 percent of total full-time enrollment in 1975, as compared to 42.9 percent in 1974. This apparent decline in representation of women in higher education enrollment is too slight to discuss
(especially in a preliminary report) but it can safely be said that it
does not represent progress.

2. Doctoral Degrees: With respect to doctorates awarded,
the latest figures indicate that women received 15.8 percent of all
doctorates in 1972; the previous peacetime peak was 15.4 percent in
1930. In 40 years the progress here amounted to less than .5 percent.

3. Professional Degrees: Women received over 10 percent of
degrees in medicine in 1950, but were just below 5 percent in 1955.
Although the trend has been positive since then, the 1972 percentage
falls short of 10 percent. Thus in 20 years progress has been negative.

In law no strictly comparable figures on women's degrees are
available before 1955. Although the trend has been generally rising
since that year, when women received under 4 percent of such degrees, there have been declines as well: from 3.5 percent in 1955
to 2.5 percent in 1960 and 3.2 percent in 1965. In 1971 women received 7.1 percent of law degrees; in 1972 only 7 percent. Here
also progress has been uncertain.

As the figures and above text indicate, then, women have not
come such a long, long, way after all.

THE ROLE OF EDUCATIONAL LEADERS IN IMPROVING
OPPORTUNITIES FOR WOMEN

Moreover, there is no evidence of commitment by the leaders
of American education to equal representation of women in higher-
level paths within the education system. For example, the fiscal

year 1971 report of the U.S. commissioner of education offers a
guide to educators nationwide in helping young people with their
career plans, in the following manner:

> For "Joe Carver" and "Jane Simpson," who show
> an early interest in things scientific, study of
> these 15 major career fields provides by grade 6
> a rudimentary knowledge of their career possibil-
> ities. Class field trips to marine laboratories,
> factories, and construction sites help to make the
> world seem real.
>   Early in junior high school both youngsters,
> after talking at length with their parents, teach-
> ers, and guidance counselor, make a tentative
> career choice. While they can change their mind
> at any time, both decide to plan toward a career
> in the environmental sciences. Joe is thinking
> about forest conservation; Jane, about water pol-
> lution control. Both plan to go to college.
>   By the time they reach senior high, Joe and
> Jane are taking the usual biology, chemistry, and
> other scientific prerequisites for college. But
> they are also getting practical experience. By
> school arrangement, Joe works two afternoons a
> week with the rangers in a nearby national forest.
> During this experience he becomes greatly inter-
> ested in rock formations and the composition of
> the earth. Jane works with the local water author-
> ity, learning how to take water samples from the
> lake that supplies the city's drinking water and
> how to test them.
>   Joe does indeed go on to the State university,
> changing directions slightly and graduating as a
> geologist. Jane, having had some trouble with
> college-prep physics and biology in high school,
> opts for a two-year postsecondary education at
> the community college. She stays in the career
> field of her choice, however, and becomes a
> biochemical technician, analyzing the pollutants
> that find their way into water supplies. [7]

We all want to give Joe his chance--but must we put down Jane?
   We can be fairly confident that Joe and Jane themselves, and
their high school contemporaries, are not likely to read this type of
putdown that relegates Jane, on the basis of no supporting evidence,

to a lifetime in the "blocked lower ranks" (Everett Hughes' term) of
paraprofessionals, following exposure to a brief technical program
at the local community college (if indeed she can win admittance to
one of the few places that may be provided in "women's programs"
in that institution). But the unsupported statement of the commissioner of education is indeed read by local high school superintendents, principals, faculties, and guidance counselors who receive
the message that Jane should not be encouraged to aspire to the
major or research universities. (As we indicated earlier, the few
young women who take physical science courses report higher percentages of As and Bs than do high school boys in those courses; the
lower SAT average scores for girls as compared to boys reflects the
distribution of courses taken by each sex, not the distribution of
ability.)

   Those who have read Pygmalion in the Classroom by Rosenthal
and Jacobson[8] recognize the impact of expectations on performance,
which affects the self-confidence and aspiration of the student as well
as the judgment of the instructor. If the secretary of education ex-
pects Jane to go to the two-year or "other four-year" college, his
prediction will have an effect on high school programs, guidance
counseling, teacher encouragement, Jane's resulting aspiration
level, and the decisions of university admissions officers.

   Let us also look at the future chances of increasing women's
percentage enrollment in top-ranking universities from another
angle, that is, we should consider any plans that are being made by
the leaders of such institutions. Harvard is perhaps the leading
American university, although this venerable institution has not led
in opening up opportunities for women. What do Harvard administrators envision with respect to the future sex composition of undergraduate enrollment?

   In response to growing concern among students and some faculty, in 1974 President Bok set up a committee headed by Professor
Strauch to look into the Harvard-Radcliffe relationship, the sex ratio
of entering classes, and financial aid policies for students of each
sex. The Strauch Committee Report is an intensive examination of
these issues. The report recommends discontinuance of Harvard's
present 5 men:2 women undergraduate ratio and the establishment
instead of an "equal access admission" policy under which "applicants
are evaluated on the basis of their academic, extracurricular and
personal qualifications independent of sex." Financial aid would be
awarded equally to individuals of either sex who are admitted.[9]

   The percentage of women expected to be among freshmen admitted under such a policy is reflected in this comment: "Other universities similar to Harvard with a tradition of equal access admissions now have a 1.5:1 ratio; we expect similar progress here within

a reasonable period."[10] Thus equal representation of women among
undergraduates at the top-ranking institutions is not on the horizon;
competitive underadmission of women remains one of the key characteristics of "selectivity."[11]

For the Harvard class of 1978 there were more than twice as
many men as women applicants (7,800 to 3,400), reflecting not only
the lower self-esteem of women, but the less-active Radcliffe recruiting (coupled possibly with lack of encouragement by some high
school administrators who may have read the 1971 report of the secretary of education). The Strauch report points to the problem of
increasing the "pool" of women applicants with high math SAT scores
"at least until there have been fundamental changes in women's interests throughout the secondary school system."[12] Yet of the 188
women applicants for the 1978 class with math SAT scores over 750,
Harvard admitted 103, not much more than half; and of the 138 women
with verbal SAT scores in that range, admitted 64, or less than half.
(The same, or lower, percent of male applicants were admitted--but
of a base more than twice as large.) If in fact the pool of Harvard
women applicants had been as large as that of men, with the score
distribution as shown, there would have been just about as many
women as men with verbal scores over 700 and over 750.

There were 1,000 women in the national pool with SAT verbal
scores over 750 (1,300 men) and 1,600 women with SAT math scores
over 750 (8,300 men), the latter disparity reflecting the sex distribution of advanced high school math courses noted earlier.[13]

Thus there is no lack of brilliant women "worthy" to be admitted to Harvard and other "research universities." In this connection, and because the myth of academic inferiority of women persists, we should recognize explicitly here the fears of many (women
as well as men) that insistence on equal admission of the sexes,
that is, 1:1, will mean that less-qualified women will be admitted
"out of turn" ahead of better-qualified men. "Equal merit" is urged
as the criterion for admission to top-ranking schools. Who could
deny the principle of equal merit? Or for that matter, who can de-
fine it?

The admissions process at all institutions of higher education,
from the best to the worst in terms of academic "quality," public as
well as private, is not generally open to public scrutiny. It is well
understood, however, within the academic community, to represent
a subjective judgment of the overall potential of applicants. It is
not, and never has been, a simple reading down a list of scores on
college entrance examinations, ranked in descending order. For example, the Strauch Committee Report indicated that no more than 10
percent of the typical entering class at Harvard would be classed as
"scholars," with an additional 30-40 percent showing "unusual

academic potential." "The balance of the class should provide diversity of talent, background and strengths," combined with strong academic potential.[14] That is, 50-60 percent of Harvard's freshmen are chosen for their "strengths," which may lie in the fields of music, literature, or sports, or may receive preference as sons of alumni, members of disadvantages minorities, or for a variety of other reasons. Thus the argument that admission of equal numbers of women undergraduates would represent a deterioration of admissions standards which now are based on objective "scores," or measurable "merit," is simply not true. Admission to top-ranking institutions is not a contest, but an evaluation. In such an evaluation it is difficult for predominantly male admissions committees, however honest their intent, to recognize the strengths of women candidates, however high-scoring. Awareness of the economic payoff to predominantly male "selective" institutions is not likely to be explicit.

Thus, the continuing lower percent of women admitted to the "research universities" represents a decision by these institutions to recruit women less vigorously, and to admit them in lesser numbers, rather than being the inevitable result of lower-caliber women applicants. Over the past decade (and in earlier years) women have been a minority of college-bound high school seniors taking the SAT college entrance examinations, and presumably of applicants to college; only in 1974 did their numbers reach equality with men among examination-takers. Obviously there could not be numerical equality of the sexes in institutions of all types when the total woman applicant pool was smaller. But the distribution of women among all types of institutions has been at odds with the expected result of the distribution of academic ability among the sexes entering college. Because of past societal curtailment of aspiration (see Chapter 2), a brighter group of girls (brighter because smaller in number, taken from the top of the high school population) have applied for college admission, together with a larger group of boys, with a wider range of academic ability.

Because of multiple applications by both sexes to several institutions, as well as reluctance of institutions to reveal admissions data, we cannot, except in isolated instances, find reported lower "scores" for entering men as compared to women. But the logic of the distribution of academic qualifications among the applicants of both sexes dictates that it is institutions of less prestige and "quality" that should have been unable to admit matching numbers of the sexes; the top-level research universities would have had no difficulty in this regard. As Table 1.1 indicated, the reverse has been the case.

As this study has sought to demonstrate throughout, it is not only in academic education beyond high school that women have been

underrepresented. Figure 5.3 permits a judgment also on progress
in vocational training for women. Although the U.S. Department of
Education ceased collection of enrollment by sex in postsecondary
programs after 1969, in its annual summary of state reports, more
recent data from subareas indicate that women remain a minority.
Preliminary results of the 1974 Office for Civil Rights study of public postsecondary area vocational schools show men as 60 percent of
the enrollment in these tax-supported facilities, with two-thirds of
men students in technical and trades and industry programs, while
over two-thirds of enrolled women were in business programs and
health fields. Similarly, the NCES survey of noncollegiate postsecondary schools with occupational programs showed women to be
only 41 percent of 1973-74 enrollment in public institutions, with
women a very high percent in health, home economics, and office,
and men similarly very high in technical and trades and industry
programs.

In apprenticeship programs, Representative Green cited an
estimate of women's representation in the late 1960s as 1 percent;
the 1974 report of the Bureau of Apprentice Training shows women
as .9 percent of registered apprentices, which cannot be construed
as progress.

In the federally funded Manpower programs, where figures are
available since the 1963 inception, women have been declining as a
percent of trainees for five or more years. In institutional training,
women's representation peaked in 1968, at almost half the total
(44.6 percent); in fiscal year 1974, women were about one-third
(33.6 percent) of trainees. In on-the-job training, the peak representation of women was in fiscal year 1969, when women were about
one-third of the total; in fiscal year 1974, women were a little better
than one-fifth (21.8 percent).

In both academic and vocational education, the adverse effects
on the status of women of such denial of equal opportunity for improving skills is not just the frustration of women denied admission.
Also for those women admitted to such education programs, the very
fact of minority status inhibits women students' self-confidence and
the encouragement of ability by (predominantly male) faculty.

This study has sought to explain the persistence of discrimination against women in entry into professional and skilled employment.
We have noted (see Tables 1.3 and 1.4) that occupations in which
women are the majority of workers tend to be low-paid--teacher,
nurse, secretary, sales clerk. Men in these fields, while earning
more than the women, are likely to earn less than men in other occupations.[15] Considering this, we cannot find it surprising that
male educators and administrators and union leaders--who control
the entry gate--are unwilling to admit women.

By admitting women to one university--or to one skilled trade--
while other schools and unions, of similar rank and prestige, continued to exclude them, the guardians of the "entry gate"--graduate,
professional, or vocational schools--would lower the rank, prestige,
and earnings of occupations from which their own incomes are derived. It is simply a rational decision of men (who throughout life
have been expected to provide the principal support for their families) to protect the welfare of their own families by keeping women
out. "One of the eternal conflicts of which life is made up," said
Justice Oliver Wendell Homes, "is that between the effort of every
man to get the most he can for his services, and that of society . . .
to get his services for the least possible return."[16] Therefore we
cannot find it surprising that the leaders of our major colleges and
universities are unwilling to "sink in the scale" by admitting more
women. Admitting women in equal numbers as undergraduates means
that eventually the university professoriate will include an equal representation of women, with presumed adverse effects on salary scales.
It means immediately that the individual university's attractiveness
(its reputation) would be diminished, in view of the general perception of women as inferior creatures. This would then diminish public and private aid, grants, and contracts, since individual or corporate or governmental funds would seek better investment in some
other institution with a higher proportion of male undergraduates.
Thus there is no economic penalty incurred by faculty and administration who have a "taste for discrimination" in Becker's model;
rather, the exclusion of women carries with it the promise of present
and future economic advantage for the decision makers, faculty, and
administration. To rely on high-sounding statements of the offending
institutions as to future movement toward equal admission is to ignore
the economic realities.

With respect to undergraduate admissions, Harvard's equal-
access plan will leave admissions decisions to the same discretion-
ary and discriminatory choices that have prevailed in the past. Given
the economic incentives to faculty and administration noted in Chapter
4, the persistent effort to lure the best male candidates may have
several likely effects on the admissions practices of top universities
and colleges adopting equal-access plans:

1. The women admitted will (as is true now) come from higher-
income families so that the drain on university resources will be
minimized. Women from lower- or moderate-income families will
continue to have lesser chances for admission to those institutions
offering the best opportunities for advanced study and professional
or governmental careers.

2. Women admitted will be those oriented toward "less profit-
able" departments--English, modern languages--that is, those where
male enrollment is below average. For example, both Princeton and
Williams found "they could admit women at a marginal educational
cost per student that was below their tuition and fee charges" through
more intensive utilization of faculty and facilities in particular departments.[17] (No mention is made of employment opportunities in
these fields subsequent to graduation.)

3. Finally, at those universities where the equal-access approach has been adopted, such policies have "yielded at best a 60/40
ratio"--that is, three undergraduate men for every two women admitted.

Institutions of higher education, both top-ranked and those that
follow the leader, are more likely to endorse the principle of equal
admissions of the sexes than to put such principles into practice;
competitive underadmission of women has an economic payoff.

In vocational education, the male vocational education administrators, faculty, and union leaders are even more directly threat-
ened by the entry of women into skilled trades. In contrast to employers (administrators) in higher education, who themselves derive
higher income from exclusionary policies, industrial employers perceive no economic advantage from discriminatory training policies.
Indeed, as Becker pointed out, they must pay to indulge a "taste for
discrimination." This leads to a well-founded fear among the guardians of the entry gate that if women are admitted to training, cost-
conscious employers may in fact prefer to hire them. Union leaders
who have fought lifelong the weary fight to maintain the pay scale of
their trades relative to other occupations cannot lightly view the admission of women to their ranks. Will the skilled worker in this
trade lose his bargaining power, when "even a woman" can tighten a
bolt or rivet a seam? The associated vocational faculty, and state
and local administrators in the educational field, are equally aware
of the problems created by funding training programs "for the girls."
Thus here also it would be premature to assume from the establishment of a few "outreach" programs that equality of educational opportunity is already won.

The Vocational Education division of the U.S. Department of
Education forecasts the infinitesimal rise in female enrollment in
postsecondary vocational education from 39.3 percent in 1970 to
40.0 percent in 1977. This less-than-dramatic increase reflects,
among other changes, a decline in women's percentage of vocational
enrollment in technical (from 9.8 percent in 1972 to 9.0 percent in
1977), as well as a rise in trades and industry (11.7 percent in 1972,
to 13.0 percent in 1977).[18] Clearly, there is yet some distance to
travel.

If the resistance of decision makers in higher education and vocational education to admission of women does indeed reflect a reasonable fear that any pioneering university or college or vocational program or trade union will suffer an economic penalty-- lower income for faculty and administration--some solution must be found to minimize any such economic dislocations. All related institutions must be induced to move toward equal admissions simultaneously, by changing the present economic payoffs to economic penalties. If all universities accept women equally, no one school becomes identified as a "weaker" institution; all skilled trades must be equally open to women, so that wage differentials based on skill remain relatively unchanged. Federal and state action must be invoked to make discrimination in admissions more costly to university, vocational school, and trade union.

Suggested legislative and other action programs are proposed in the following pages. In some cases, action by organized women's groups may be more effective; however, particularly at the local level, individual concerned parents can persuade school officials to change policies on texts or courses of study in order to provide more opportunities for both sexes to develop a wide range of talents.

Some may believe political action unnecessary or even extreme. Americans often assume that America is in the forefront of social and economic progress, since we led for so many years in the areas of individual rights and economic prosperity of our citizens. Today, however, more than American women realize, this country is lagging behind others in areas affecting women. Even in the small African country of Guinea-Bissau, which became independent only in 1973, a young woman contrasted her status with that of her mother:

> My mother was not free. If she wanted to do anything at all, she had to ask my father's permission. Her work was very hard--cooking rice, fishing, pounding rice, feeding her children, keeping house and working in the fields.
>
> I first heard about women's rights at the beginning of the APIGC mobilizations. I understood what was being said immediately. Equality is possible and necessary. Today I work together with men and have more responsibility than many men.[19]

Francoise Giroud, Secretary of State for the Status of Women in France, recently commented:

> I agree that the place of women in the world-- and especially in the U.S.--is detestable.

> Believe it or not, it is worse in the States from
> a salary standpoint than it is in France. The
> percentage of women doctors, judges, and en-
> gineers is considerably higher in France than
> it is in the United States, where it is ridiculous-
> ly low. France already has a comprehensive,
> free day care program for children aged $2\frac{1}{2}$ to 6. [20]

Thus the suggestions on the following pages to achieve equal
educational opportunity may also serve to bring the United States
once more among the leading nations seeking to establish social and
political equality for all citizens. (Detailed suggestions for action
at the local, state, and federal level by voters and taxpayers will be
found in Appendix I. A general discussion of effective routes to
remedial action is given in the following pages.)

ROUTES TO CHANGE

We have seen that opportunities for young women in undergraduate education, and in training for skilled trades after the high
school years, are less than for equally-qualified young men.

We have seen that tax-derived funds, at local, state, and federal levels support this discriminatory system. Although we have
concentrated on undergraduate education as the fundamental area,
we should note that enrollments are even more lopsided in favor of
young men at graduate and professional schools (see Table 1.2)
where tax-derived support is even greater per enrolled student.
Thus we have considerably understated the extent to which young
women and their parents, as well as all taxpayers, are financing the
education of young men at the expense of young women.

We have seen that such inequality of educational opportunity
leads to the relegation of women to lower-paid, unskilled employment for a working life that covers 20 or 30 years.

In the interest of changing the pattern of discrimination against
women in postsecondary education, young women and their parents,
as well as all fair-minded taxpayers, may use three principal methods: (1) economic incentives for equal admissions, (2) political incentives for equal admissions, and (3) persuasion.

Economic Incentives for Equal Admissions

1. If the discriminatory actions of educators, administrators,
and union officials are to a large extent determined by their

understandable interest in protecting their own economic welfare, we should use that same economic motive to end such discrimination. Tax dollars are now distributed so as to reward those undergraduate institutions that most discriminate against women. Therefore, we must change the payoffs. Let us instead penalize discrimination by withholding tax-funded grants, contracts, and institutional funds for scholarships from those undergraduate institutions that do not immediately begin, and within five years reach, a policy of equal admissions to undergraduate status.

2. Likewise, vocational institutions and union organizations that delay their implementation of Title IX (see Appendix A) should be denied MDTA and other federal funds, as well as state support. Employers who do not provide equal access to on-the-job training or similar training programs should also be denied federal funds.

3. A "Mother's Bill for Educational Opportunity" similar to the G.I. Bill should be enacted. Since World War II interested veterans have been eligible for federal tuition payments and subsistence grants to assist them in improving their education levels and thus their job opportunities. These tax-derived funds are given because such youth have guaranteed the survival of this country and its citizens, often at considerable sacrifice. In a different but equally real sense, women who are mothers have guaranteed the survival of this country, and should be rewarded rather than penalized for this contribution. Day care should be provided, as well as tuition and subsistence, to enable young women having the requisite interest and ability to improve their job eligibility. Such a measure would incidentally provide financial assistance to struggling institutions of higher education, or vocational schools, and at the same time serve the country well by improving the quality of the labor force.

Political Incentives for Equal Admissions

1. We must have education administrators at state and local levels who support equal admissions. Varying by state, some top education officials are elected and some are appointed. Officials making appointments, and officials who are directly elected, are generally responsive to voter wishes.

2. Since commencement ceremonies often begin: "By the power vested in me by the state . . . to award degrees, . . ." state education officials must withdraw the degree-granting power from those institutions that continue to discriminate in undergraduate admission.

3. Federal congressmen and senators must be elected who will amend Title IX to include all undergraduate institutions, private as well as public.

4. Vocational programs in public and private nonprofit institutions of higher education, and in public postsecondary vocational education, must be denied state education department approval (and thus their function) until evidence of vigorous recruiting is begun to equalize admissions and enrollments by program and school.

5. MDTA (now CETA) and other federally funded training programs must be continually monitored to insure that women in need of training are not shunted into training for unskilled, dead-end jobs.

Persuasion

1. At the local level, young women, their parents, and all fair-minded taxpayers and voters can confer with teachers, principals, school superintendents, vocational administrators, and similar decision makers on the problem of sex discrimination in order to end the use of sex-stereotyped texts, to open up enrollment in mathematics courses, shop courses, physics courses, and athletic programs. Although equality of treatment in the latter areas is guaranteed by Title IX, expressions of concern by interested voters and taxpayers will do a good deal to convince local authorities of the need for strong commitment to equality of educational opportunity.

2. Support for men and women political candidates who advocate such equal educational opportunity for all youth will underscore the need for prompt action.

3. Universities that led in the development of the "new physics" in response to the challenge of Sputnik may likewise want to add their voices and expertise so as to end sex-discriminatory patterns of elementary and secondary education, in order to facilitate the ending of such discrimination in higher education and postsecondary vocational education.

SUMMARY

If, as a result of legislation and action suggested above (also see Appendix I), American women achieve equal access to professions of law and medicine, become welders and carpenters, scientists and senators--what then? Will either women or society benefit by such a transformation?

As with any advance in human freedom and potential, society must benefit by the development of human talent and powers. The benefits, however, will be more than the increased productivity of better educated and more highly skilled women, and more than the satisfaction of achievement by individual women. The benefits to American men will be substantial.

The lack of economic partnership between the sexes in modern industrial society costs the American man in many ways. Married men have carried the burden of American production since farming ceased to be the principal economic occupation early in this century. Hypertensive, ulcer-ridden American men are expected to work full time, full year, until they retire or die. If girls and women are given equal educational opportunity, they will take on a greater share of responsibility for family income. Even into this century, farm women were equal economic partners in providing food and clothing for the family. A larger joint income would provide greater security for both men and women in marriage; the male partner would be freer to venture into new fields, to take a "sabbatical year" (as some women may now), to see more of his family.

Both society and individual men and women have suffered from the different and inferior education given girls and women. If young women join with their parents and other taxpayers to insist on equal opportunities for development of talent, regardless of sex, we need not anticipate utopia. We can be confident that our material welfare as a nation will be improved, as a more productive labor force is developed by the education system. But, much more, we will have a society that will gain immeasurably from the greater job satisfaction and life satisfaction of productive individuals using their talents to the fullest.

NOTES

1. Alden Thresher, College Admissions and the Public Interest (New York: College Entrance Examination Board, 1966), p. 58.

2. Humphrey Doermann, Crosscurrents in College Admissions (New York: Teachers College Press, Columbia University, 1968). Testimony of John F. Morse, Director of the Commission on Federal Relations of the American Council on Education, 1964, p. 110.

3. S. Freedberg, Acting Chairman, Fine Arts, Harvard University, quoted in Harvard Crimson, March 27, 1973, p. 1.

4. U.S. Congress, Congressional Record-House, H-10365, November 4, 1971 (see Appendix G).

5. Edie Van Horn, United Auto Workers, quoted in "At Large," by Mike Barnicle, Boston Globe, July 2, 1975.

6. U.S. Department of Health, Education, and Welfare, Summary Table, Aggregate U.S. Enrollment Fall 1974 and Fall 1975 (preliminary data) (Washington, D.C., December 5, 1975).

7. U.S. Department of Health, Education, and Welfare, Annual Report of the Commissioner of Education, 1971 (Washington, D.C., 1972), p. 65.

8. Robert Rosenthal and Lenore Jacobson, Pygmalion in the Classroom (New York: Holt, Rinehart, and Winston, 1968).

9. Harvard University and Radcliffe College, Report of the Committee to Consider Aspects of the Harvard-Radcliffe Relationship That Affect Administrative Arrangements, Admissions, Financial Aid, and Educational Policy (Strauch Report) (Cambridge, Mass., February 26, 1975).

10. Ibid., p. 15.

11. Alexander Astin, Predicting Academic Performance in College: Selectivity data on 2300 American colleges (New York: The Free Press, 1971).

12. Strauch Report, op. cit., p. A4-10.

13. Ibid., p. A4-9.

14. Ibid., p. A2-2.

15. U.S. Department of Labor, Monthly Labor Review, August 1974, p. 50.

16. Oliver W. Holmes, quoted in American Labor and Manpower Policy, ed. Ronald Wykstra and Eleanor Stevens (New York: Odyssey Press, 1970), p. 52.

17. Carnegie Commission on Higher Education, Opportunities for Women in Higher Education (New York: McGraw-Hill, 1973), p. 52.

18. U.S. Department of Health, Education, and Welfare, Division of Vocational and Technical Education, Vocational Education Information I, Section I (Washington, D.C., 1973), Table 3 (see Appendix H).

19. Stephanie Urdang, "African Sex Roles Changing," Boston University Daily Free Press, September 27, 1974, p. 1.

20. Francoise Giroud, Boston Globe, October 29, 1974, p. 20.

TITLE IX OF EDUCATION AMENDMENTS OF 1972

Public Law 92-318
92nd Congress, S. 659
June 23, 1972

AN ACT

To amend the Higher Education Act of 1965, the Vocational
Education Act of 1963, the General Education Provisions Act (creat-
ing a National Foundation for Postsecondary Education and a National
Institute of Education), the Elementary and Secondary Education Act
of 1965, Public Law 874, Eighty-first Congress, and related Acts,
and for other purposes.

Title IX--Prohibition of Sex Discrimination

Sex Discrimination Prohibited

Sec. 901. (a) No person in the United States shall, on the basis
of sex, be excluded from participation in, be denied the benefits of,
or be subjected to discrimination under any education program or
activity receiving Federal financial assistance, except that:

> (1) in regard to admissions to educational institu-
> tions, this section shall apply only to institutions of
> vocational education, professional education, and
> graduate higher education, and to public institutions
> of undergraduate higher education;
> (2) in regard to admissions to educational in-
> stitutions, this section shall not apply (A) for one
> year from the date of enactment of this Act, nor for
> six years after such date in the case of an educa-
> tional institution which has begun the process of
> changing from being an institution which admits only
> students of one sex to being an institution which ad-
> mits students of both sexes, but only if it is carry-
> ing out a plan for such a change which is approved
> by the Commissioner of Education or (B) for seven
> years from the date an educational institution begins

the process of changing from being an institution
which admits only students of only one sex to being
an institution which admits students of both sexes,
but only if it is carrying out a plan for such a
change which is approved by the Commissioner of
Education, whichever is the later;

(3) this section shall not apply to an educational
institution which is controlled by a religious organi-
zation if the application of this subsection would not
be consistent with the religious tenets of such or-
ganization;

(4) this section shall not apply to an educational
institution whose primary purpose is the training of
individuals for the military services of the United
States, or the merchant marine; and

(5) in regard to admissions this section shall
not apply to any public institution of undergraduate
higher education which is an institution that traditionally and continually from its establishment has
had a policy of admitting only students of one sex.

(b) Nothing contained in subsection (a) of this section shall be
interpreted to require any educational institution to grant preferential or disparate treatment to the members of one sex on account of
an imbalance which may exist with respect to the total number or
percentage of persons of that sex participating in or receiving the
benefits of any federally supported program or activity, in comparison with the total number or percentage of persons of that sex in any
community, State, section, or other area: Provided, that this subsection shall not be construed to prevent the consideration in any
hearing or proceeding under this title of statistical evidence tending
to show that such an imbalance exists with respect to the participation in, or receipt of the benefits of, any such program or activity
by the members of one sex.

(c) For purposes of this title an educational institution means
any public or private preschool, elementary, or secondary school,
or any institution of vocational, professional, or higher education,
except that in the case of an educational institution composed of more
than one school, college, or department which are administratively
separate units, such term means each such school, college, or department.

Federal Administrative Enforcement

Sec. 902. Each Federal department and agency which is em-
powered to extend Federal financial assistance to any education

program or activity, by way of grant, loan, or contract other than a contract of insurance or guaranty, is authorized and directed to effectuate the provisions of section 901 with respect to such program or activity by issuing rules, regulations, or orders of general applicability which shall be consistent with achievement of the objectives of the statute authorizing the financial assistance in connection with which the action is taken. . . .

REPRESENTATION OF WOMEN IN APPRENTICESHIPS,
OCCUPATIONAL PROGRAMS OF HIGHER EDUCATION,
AND MANPOWER TRAINING PROGRAMS

TABLE B.1

Total and Female Apprentices, by Trade or Craft,
in Selected States, 1972*

State/Trade or Craft	Number of Programs	Number of Apprentices Total	Number of Apprentices Female
Arkansas	32	332	0
California	318	26,385	76
Automotive mechanic	10	630	1
Butcher-meat cutter	16	1,060	2
Carpenter	22	12,034	3
Painter	23	1,688	28
Plumber-pipe fitter	36	1,824	1
Printing pressman	10	174	6
Miscellaneous trades	11	724	6
Colorado	80	2,421	4
Machinist	5	31	1
Delaware	19	253	4
Florida	99	5,955	4
Carpenter	9	1,894	1
Plumber-pipe fitter	15	1,140	1
Printing pressman	3	22	2
Illinois	277	11,396	27
Bookbinder	4	116	4
Carpenter	16	1,818	1
Lithographer	3	1,688	14
Printing pressman	20	285	8
Kansas	22	448	0
Massachusetts	63	3,133	13
Carpenter	13	501	1
Printing pressman	8	173	12

(continued)

State/Trade or Craft	Number of Programs	Number of Apprentices Total	Female
Michigan	704	9,305	12
Bricklayer	9	110	3
Printing pressman	5	168	1
Tool and die maker	119	1,219	1
Mississippi	45	814	2
Electrical worker	10	236	2
Nevada	35	845	4
New Jersey	183	2,838	19
Printing pressman	7	56	4
Miscellaneous trades	5	50	15
New York	210	9,619	34
Electrical worker	36	3,401	1
Printing pressman	12	372	1
Ohio	396	7,243	16
Electrical worker	72	2,019	1
Iron worker	12	352	2
Printing pressman	13	161	9
Tool and die maker	45	367	2
Oklahoma	26	780	1
Pennsylvania	253	5,950	81
Bookbinder	6	93	25
Printing pressman	23	310	52
South Carolina	28	285	1
Texas	126	5,691	10
Carpenter	17	1,275	2
Painter	3	128	1
Printing pressman	14	196	5
Vermont	10	140	0
Wyoming	13	277	0

*Separate trade or craft statistics are shown only for those trades in which females were reported.

Note: Reports are required from each joint labor-management apprenticeship committee subject to Title VII that has: five or more apprentices in its entire program; and at least one employer sponsoring the program who has 25 or more employees; and at least one union sponsoring the program that operates a hiring hall or has 25 or more members. (The numbers reported above represent about one-third of all registered apprentices in 1972.)

Source: Equal Employment Opportunity Commission, Apprenticeship Information Report EEO-2 (Washington, D.C., 1972).

TABLE B.2

Apprentice Registrations Actions,* Calendar Year 1974

Region/State	Beginning of Period	During Period			End of Period			
		Added	Cancelled	Completed	Apprens.	Minorities	Female	Veterans
U.S. total	280,965	112,830	56,292	46,454	291,049	45,808†	2,562†	96,634†
Region I – total	15,643	6,869	3,552	2,936	16,024	1,208	130	7,073
Connecticut	5,914	3,099	1,434	844	6,735	517	48	2,745
Maine	1,177	426	311	188	1,104	2	2	607
Massachusetts	6,382	2,246	1,135	1,496	5,997	588	46	2,729
New Hampshire	342	169	61	91	359	5	9	138
Rhode Island	676	365	138	153	750	5	12	294
Vermont	1,152	564	473	164	1,079	3	13	560
Region II – total	30,066	8,523	5,720	5,976	26,893	4,730	290	9,457
New Jersey	8,303	2,451	567	1,280	8,907	1,619	45	2,179
New York	20,565	5,397	4,736	4,293	16,933	2,060	116	7,197
Puerto Rico	1,136	675	417	403	991	989	129	68
Virgin Islands	62	0	0	0	62	62	0	13
District of Columbia	3,500	1,533	1,006	444	3,583	916	33	1,049
Region III – total	24,163	11,215	4,831	4,063	26,484	2,390	479	7,464
Delaware	1,279	362	207	211	1,223	100	6	358
Maryland	3,443	2,085	686	563	4,279	547	62	1,649
Pennsylvania	10,729	3,773	1,430	1,963	11,109	759	24	1,933
Virginia	7,574	4,387	2,222	1,096	8,643	928	365	3,439
West Virginia	1,138	608	286	230	1,230	56	22	85
Region IV – total	38,851	14,323	7,874	4,269	41,031	4,650	272	14,195
Alabama	3,038	1,436	315	451	3,708	617	21	774
Florida	11,771	4,251	3,017	1,496	11,509	1,027	59	4,125
Georgia	4,246	1,664	806	496	4,608	838	71	850
Kentucky	3,301	1,549	958	599	3,293	318	14	1,112
Mississippi	1,567	1,809	1,116	222	2,038	416	67	376
North Carolina	7,906	50	21	8	7,927	398	12	5,069
South Carolina	2,209	1,358	1,077	170	2,320	301	4	469
Tennessee	4,813	2,206	564	827	5,628	735	24	1,420

158

Region V - total	66,827	23,754	8,275	12,322	69,984	7,688	633	19,271
Illinois	15,476	4,201	1,159	2,908	15,610	2,388	45	3,193
Indiana	6,201	2,625	750	1,126	6,950	790	67	2,123
Michigan	15,053	6,068	2,169	2,226	16,726	2,159	117	3,750
Minnesota	6,530	2,363	1,057	1,298	6,538	209	12	2,871
Ohio	15,231	5,428	2,010	3,121	15,231	1,668	88	4,194
Wisconsin	8,336	3,069	1,130	1,643	8,632	474	304	3,140
Region VI - total	20,568	12,480	4,746	3,077	25,225	6,223	195	8,352
Arkansas	1,375	654	251	202	1,576	225	2	527
Louisiana	5,119	2,311	946	599	6,385	1,554	88	2,686
New Mexico	1,528	328	446	225	1,685	890	3	371
Oklahoma	1,927	1,166	580	323	2,190	386	6	673
Texas	10,619	7,021	2,523	1,728	13,389	3,168	96	4,095
Region VII - total	9,411	4,052	1,293	2,025	10,145	1,227	79	3,293
Iowa	2,254	1,244	389	531	2,578	196	7	983
Kansas	1,172	393	143	143	1,279	160	9	283
Missouri	4,751	1,865	543	1,065	5,018	747	52	1,560
Nebraska	1,224	550	218	286	1,270	124	11	467
Region VIII - total	8,584	4,976	2,092	1,361	10,107	1,137	77	3,320
Colorado	3,106	1,493	879	557	3,163	692	11	638
Montana	1,623	1,007	388	270	1,977	108	47	923
North Dakota	789	427	195	111	910	32	4	278
South Dakota	555	166	90	49	582	21	3	85
Utah	1,962	1,575	444	264	2,829	217	7	1,142
Wyoming	544	308	96	110	646	67	5	254
Region IX - total	51,120	18,406	14,249	7,701	47,576	14,325	256	17,217
Arizona	4,407	1,655	1,145	755	4,162	1,287	10	1,549
California	40,790	14,305	11,891	6,012	37,192	8,996	231	13,692
Guam	242	48	40	36	214	214	4	42
Hawaii	3,921	1,920	883	615	4,343	3,532	6	1,217
Nevada	1,760	478	290	283	1,665	296	5	717
Region X - total	12,232	6,699	2,654	2,280	13,997	1,314	118	5,943
Alaska	748	491	5	119	1,069	276	3	305
Idaho	1,071	528	197	152	1,250	76	15	402
Oregon	4,538	2,452	966	957	5,067	185	21	2,572
Washington	5,875	3,228	1,440	1,052	6,611	777	79	2,664

*U.S. totals for Bureau of Apprenticeship and Training and State Apprenticeship Councils.

†Minimum figures. Characteristic data not available on all apprentices.

Source: Computer printout distributed by U.S. Department of Labor, Bureau of Apprenticeship and Training, March 1976.

TABLE B.3

Formal Awards Based on Organized Occupational Curriculums at the Technical or Semiprofessional
Level in Institutions of Higher Education, by Length and Type of Curriculum and by Sex
(United States and outlying areas, 1970-71)

Curriculum	All Awards			Awards Based on Organized Occupational Curriculums of--					
				At Least 2 Years but Less Than 4 Years			At Least 1 Year but Less Than 2 Years		
	Total	Men	Women	Total	Men	Women	Total	Men	Women
All curriculums	153,549	83,380	70,169	124,093	71,527	52,566	29,456	11,853	17,603
Science and engineering-related curriculums	87,728	50,882	36,846	68,213	42,123	26,090	19,515	8,759	10,756
Mechanical and engineering technologies	37,437	36,915	522	30,172	29,761	411	7,265	7,154	111
Mechanical engineering, general	2,560	2,538	22	2,363	2,342	21	197	196	1
Aeronautical and aviation	2,173	2,154	19	1,951	1,937	14	222	217	5
Engineering graphics	2,917	2,857	60	2,355	2,313	42	562	544	18
Architectural drafting	1,938	1,885	53	1,691	1,649	42	247	236	11
Chemical	589	485	104	547	476	71	42	9	33
Automotive	4,041	4,037	4	2,820	2,816	4	1,221	1,221	--
Diesel	721	712	9	559	550	9	162	162	--
Welding	1,097	1,090	7	475	475	--	622	615	7
Civil	1,637	1,625	12	1,577	1,565	12	60	60	--
Electronics and machine	7,851	7,826	25	7,001	6,979	22	850	847	3
Electromechanical	1,301	1,297	4	1,279	1,276	3	22	21	1
Industrial	1,657	1,637	20	1,267	1,252	15	390	385	5
Textile	155	48	107	148	42	106	7	6	1
Instrumentation	203	201	2	157	155	2	46	46	--
Mechanical	2,749	2,732	17	2,347	2,337	10	402	395	7
Nuclear	65	56	9	63	55	8	2	1	1
Construction and building	4,229	4,215	14	2,551	2,541	10	1,678	1,674	4
All other mechanical engineering technologies	1,554	1,520	34	1,021	1,001	20	533	519	14

Natural-science technologies	7,028	5,426	1,602	6,107	4,751	1,356	921	675	246
Natural science, general	656	483	173	472	305	167	184	178	6
Agriculture	2,870	2,608	262	2,734	2,487	247	136	121	15
Forestry and wildlife	1,087	1,079	8	957	949	8	130	130	--
Food services	693	462	231	455	343	112	238	119	119
Home economics	872	75	797	761	61	700	111	14	97
Marine and oceanographic	183	168	15	175	168	15	8	8	--
Laboratory, general	144	84	60	144	84	60	--	--	--
Sanitation and public health inspection	145	130	15	80	74	6	65	56	9
All other natural science technologies	378	337	41	329	288	41	49	49	--
Health services and paramedical technologies	34,518	2,911	31,607	24,370	2,455	21,915	10,148	456	9,692
Health services assistant, general	258	28	230	46	9	37	212	19	193
Dental assistant	2,191	53	2,138	685	32	653	1,506	21	1,485
Dental hygiene	2,506	17	2,489	2,461	16	2,445	45	1	44
Dental laboratory	264	171	93	227	153	74	37	18	19
Medical or biological laboratory assistant	1,335	305	1,030	1,016	281	735	319	24	295
Animal laboratory assistant	55	32	23	55	32	23	--	--	--
Radiologic	1,139	357	782	1,072	333	739	67	24	43
Nursing, R.N.	14,408	609	13,799	14,405	608	13,797	3	1	2
Nursing, practical	7,708	212	7,496	1,218	41	1,177	6,490	171	6,319
Occupational therapy	243	26	217	185	23	162	58	3	55
Surgical	244	40	204	70	26	44	174	14	160
Optical	81	73	8	81	73	8	--	--	--
Medical record	374	15	359	338	15	323	36	--	36
Medical assistant and medical office assistant	1,256	80	1,176	552	61	491	704	19	685
Inhalation therapy	570	300	270	540	290	250	30	10	20
Psychiatric	634	205	429	555	172	383	79	33	46
Electro diagnostic	22	5	17	14	4	10	8	1	7
Institutional management	176	85	91	55	40	15	121	45	76
Physical therapy	239	43	196	228	42	186	11	1	10
All other health services and paramedical technologies	815	255	560	567	204	363	248	51	197

(continued)

161

(Table B.3 continued)

| Curriculum | All Awards | | | Awards Based on Organized Occupational Curriculums of-- | | | | | |
| | | | | At Least 2 Years but Less Than 4 Years | | | At Least 1 Year but Less Than 2 Years | | |
	Total	Men	Women	Total	Men	Women	Total	Men	Women
Data-processing technologies	8,745	5,630	3,115	7,564	5,156	2,408	1,181	474	707
Data processing, general	5,027	3,302	1,725	4,698	3,087	1,611	329	215	114
Key punch operator and other input preparation	648	81	567	164	24	140	484	57	427
Computer programmer	2,149	1,554	595	1,965	1,415	550	184	139	45
Computer operator and peripheral equipment operation	387	188	199	210	130	80	177	58	119
Data processing equipment maintenance	431	429	2	431	429	2	---	---	---
All other data processing technologies	103	76	27	96	71	25	7	5	2
Nonscience- and nonengineering-related curriculums	65,821	32,498	33,323	55,880	29,404	26,476	9,941	3,094	6,847
Business and commerce technologies	51,037	23,457	27,580	43,571	22,067	21,504	7,466	1,390	6,076
Business and commerce, general	11,008	7,991	3,017	10,396	7,781	2,615	612	210	402
Accounting	5,301	3,591	1,710	4,829	3,414	1,415	472	177	295
Banking and finance	272	216	56	252	207	45	20	9	11
Marketing, distribution, purchasing, business, and industrial management	9,237	6,666	2,571	8,649	6,217	2,432	588	449	139
Secretarial	16,534	279	16,255	12,190	238	11,952	4,344	41	4,303

Personal service	1,262	78	1,184	498	22	476	764	56	708
Photography	577	516	61	529	488	41	48	28	20
Communications and broadcasting	728	527	201	723	522	201	5	5	--
Printing and lithography	512	487	25	431	420	11	81	67	14
Hotel and restaurant management	916	694	222	847	644	203	69	50	19
Transportation and public utility	324	238	86	262	203	59	62	35	27
Applied arts, graphic arts, and fine arts	2,998	1,355	1,643	2,924	1,312	1,612	74	43	31
All other business and commerce technologies	1,368	819	549	1,041	599	442	327	220	107
All other nonscience- and nonengineering-related curriculums	14,784	9,041	5,743	12,309	7,337	4,972	2,475	1,704	771
Public service related, general	277	102	175	212	92	120	65	10	55
Bible study or religion related	744	340	404	604	305	299	140	35	105
Education	3,856	589	3,267	3,351	508	2,843	505	81	424
Library assistant	471	31	440	376	30	346	95	1	94
Police, law enforcement, corrections	6,873	6,453	420	5,502	5,098	404	1,371	1,355	16
Recreation and social work related	1,146	526	620	1,121	505	616	25	21	4
Fire control	735	716	19	581	571	10	154	145	9
Public administration and management	111	96	15	84	74	10	27	22	5
Other	571	188	383	478	154	324	93	34	59

Source: U.S. Department of Health, Education, and Welfare, Digest of Education Statistics, 1974 (Washington, D.C.: Government Printing Office, 1975), Table 121, pp. 105-06.

Occupational Training of Enrollees in MDTA Training Programs,
by Type of Program, Fiscal Year 1974
(numbers in thousands)

Major Occupation Group and Selected[a] Occupations	Institutional		JOP-OJT[b]	
	Number	Percent Distribution	Number	Percent Distribution
Total	110.4	--	63.1	--
Basic education and other nonoccupational training	17.8	--	--	--
Occupational training	92.6	100.0	63.1	100.0
Professional, technical, and managerial	8.9	9.6	3.8	6.0
Architecture and engineering	1.7	1.8	.7	1.1
Medicine and health	6.6	7.1	--	--
Managers and officials[c]	--	--	1.4	2.2
Clerical and sales	19.7	21.1	7.0	11.1
Stenography, typing, filing, and related	12.8	13.8	1.9	3.0
Computing and account recording	5.5	5.9	1.1	1.7
Material and production recording	--	--	1.6	2.5
Merchandising occupations, except salespersons	--	--	.7	1.1
Service	8.9	9.7	3.9	6.2
Food and beverage preparation and service	2.7	2.9	1.8	2.9
Barbering, cosmetology, and related services	1.2	1.3	--	--
Miscellaneous personal services	2.9	3.1	.6	1.0
Protective services	1.2	1.3	--	--
Building and related services	--	--	.6	1.0
Farming, fishery, and forestry	.6	.6	.3	.5
Processing	.1	.1	3.5	5.6
Metal processing	--	--	.8	1.3
Food, tobacco, and related processing	--	--	1.0	1.6
Chemicals and synthetics processing	--	--	.8	1.3
Machine trades	20.8	22.7	16.8	26.7
Metal machining	6.0	6.5	5.9	9.4
Metalworking[c]	--	--	1.8	2.9
Mechanics and machinery repairs	13.9	15.0	4.6	7.3
Wood machinery	--	--	1.3	2.4
Textile occupations	--	--	1.6	2.5
Machine work[c]	--	--	1.3	2.1
Benchwork	3.0	3.1	8.0	12.7
Fabrication and repair of metal products	--	--	1.2	1.9
Fabrication and repair of scientific products	.2	1.2	.9	1.4
Assembly and repair of electrical equipment	1.6	1.7	2.5	4.0
Fabrication and repair of textile and leather	--	--	1.7	2.7
Structural work	27.2	29.3	15.4	24.5
Metal fabrication[c]	4.9	5.3	3.2	5.1
Welding, flame cutting, and related	11.4	12.3	1.5	2.4
Electrical assembly and repairing	2.3	2.5	1.1	1.7
Painting, plastering, and cementing	--	--	1.4	2.2
Excavating, grading, and paving	--	--	.9	1.4
Construction work[c]	5.2	5.6	6.6	10.5
Structural work[c]	13.4	14.5	--	--
Miscellaneous	3.6	3.8	4.4	7.0
Motor freight	1.6	1.7	.7	1.1
Production and distribution of utilities	--	--	1.8	2.9

[a]Data are shown separately only for those occupations in each major group with 1 percent or more of the trainees in each program.

[b]Jobs Optional/On-the-job Training. Does not include Construction Outreach enrollments.

[c]Not elsewhere classified.

Source: U.S. Department of Labor, Manpower Report of the President, 1975 (Washington, D.C., 1975), Table F-8, p. 325.

TABLE B.5

Manpower Programs Percent Distribution
of Enrollment Among Major Program Groups

Program Group	Nonminority	Blacks	Female
Skill Training[a]	27.2	15.5	18.4
Job Development[b]	8.4	8.3	6.5
Employability Development[c]	11.7	18.3	16.2
Work Experience[d]	54.5	57.4	58.3
Total	100.0	100.0	100.0

[a]Includes MDTA Institutional and on-the-job training programs.

[b]Includes Job Opportunities in the Business Sector, Public Service Careers, Public Employment Program, and Apprenticeship Outreach Program.

[c]Includes Opportunities Industrialization Center, Concentrated Employment Program, Work Incentive Program, and Job Corps.

[d]Includes Neighborhood Youth Corps-in-School, Summer, and Out-of-School programs.

Source: Reprinted with permission from C. R. Perry, B. E. Anderson, R. L. Rowan, and H. R. Northrup, The Impact of Government Manpower Programs in General and on Minorities and Women (Philadelphia: Industrial Research Unit, the Wharton School, University of Pennsylvania, 1975), p. 24. Copyright by the Trustees of the University of Pennsylvania.

APPENDIX C

WOMEN AS A PERCENTAGE OF FULL-TIME UNDERGRADUATES IN RESEARCH UNIVERSITIES, FALL 1973

State and School	Percentage
Alabama	
Public	
Auburn University, main campus	39
Arizona	
Public	
University of Arizona	44
Arkansas	
Public	
University of Arkansas, main campus	41
California	
Public	
University of California, Berkeley	40
University of California, Davis	46
University of California, Los Angeles	46
University of California, San Diego	42
Private	
California Institute of Technology	12
Stanford University	39
University of Southern California	38
Colorado	
Public	
Colorado State University	45
University of Colorado, main campus	41
Connecticut	
Public	
University of Connecticut, main campus	45
Private	
Yale University	26
District of Columbia	
Private	
Catholic University of America	46
George Washington University	42

State and School	Percentage
Florida	
Public	
Florida State University	51
University of Florida	39
Private	
University of Miami	37
Georgia	
Public	
Georgia Institute of Technology	8
University of Georgia	46
Private	
Emory University, main campus	45
Hawaii	
Public	
University of Hawaii, main campus	48
Illinois	
Public	
University of Illinois, Urbana	40
Private	
Illinois Institute of Technology	9
Northwestern University	43
University of Chicago	34
Indiana	
Public	
Purdue University, main campus	37
Indiana University, Bloomington	46
Iowa	
Public	
Iowa State University of Science and Technology	39
University of Iowa	46
Kansas	
Public	
Kansas State University of Agriculture and Applied Sciences	41
University of Kansas	43
Kentucky	
Public	
University of Kentucky	44
Louisiana	
Public	
Louisiana State University, Baton Rouge	40

State and School	Percentage
Maryland	
Public	
University of Maryland, main campus	46
Private	
Johns Hopkins University	23
Massachusetts	
Public	
University of Massachusetts, Amherst	44
Private	
Harvard University	26
Massachusetts Institute of Technology	12
Boston University	53
Brandeis University	48
Tufts University	45
Michigan	
Public	
Michigan State University	47
University of Michigan, main campus	44
Wayne State University	46
Minnesota	
Public	
University of Minnesota, Minneapolis–St. Paul	42
Mississippi	
Public	
Mississippi State University	35
Missouri	
Public	
University of Missouri, Columbia	43
Private	
Washington University	45
Nebraska	
Public	
University of Nebraska, main campus	40
New Jersey	
Public	
Rutgers University, New Brunswick	44
Private	
Princeton University	27

State and School	Percentage
New York	
Public	
State University of New York, Buffalo,	
main campus	39
Private	
Columbia University, main division	17
Cornell University, main campus	29
New York University	46
Syracuse University	46
University of Rochester	42
Yeshiva University	39
North Carolina	
Public	
North Carolina State University, Raleigh	22
University of North Carolina, Chapel Hill	40
Private	
Duke University	41
Ohio	
Public	
Ohio State University, main campus	41
University of Cincinnati, main campus	39
Private	
Case Western Reserve University	33
Oklahoma	
Public	
Oklahoma State University, main campus	39
University of Oklahoma, main campus	39
Oregon	
Public	
Oregon State University	39
University of Oregon, main campus	43
Pennsylvania	
Public	
Temple University	44
Pennsylvania State University, main campus	38
University of Pittsburgh, main campus	42
Private	
Carnegie-Mellon University	31
University of Pennsylvania	35

State and School	Percentage
Rhode Island	
Private	
Brown University	37
Tennessee	
Public	
University of Tennessee, Knoxville	40
Private	
Vanderbilt University	39
Texas	
Public	
Texas Agricultural and Mechanical University	22
University of Texas, Austin	43
Private	
Rice University	27
Utah	
Public	
University of Utah	37
Virginia	
Public	
University of Virginia, main campus	34
Virginia Polytechnic Institute and State University	32
Washington	
Public	
Washington State University	42
University of Washington	42
West Virginia	
Public	
West Virginia University, main campus	39
Wisconsin	
Public	
University of Wisconsin, Madison	44

Note: At some institutions the percent of women among total undergraduates overstates the numbers admitted to the "arts and sciences" college, from which aspiration to Ph.D. or professional study is both more likely and more possible. Women are often channeled initially or as upperclassmen to the School of Education, Nursing, and so on.

Source: James Cass and Max Birnbaum, Guide to American Colleges (New York: Harper and Row, 1972), pp. 279, 395, 446.

STEPS IN THE MERIT SCHOLARSHIP COMPETITION

The National Merit Scholarship Program, which made its first awards in 1956, completed its fifteenth annual nationwide talent search and scholarship competition in 1970.

Students enter the Merit Scholarship competition by taking the National Merit Scholarship Qualifying Test (NMSQT) in the calendar year before the one in which they complete or leave secondary school and enter college. In the 1969-70 Merit Program, the NMSQT was administered to 734,375 students in 17,256 secondary schools in the United States and its territories and in schools abroad enrolling students who are U.S. citizens.

Semifinalists

On the basis of their performance on the NMSQT, the highest-scoring students in each state and in other selection units, such as the District of Columbia and overseas schools enrolling U.S. students, qualified as Semifinalists. In the 1969-70 Merit Program, 14,677 Semifinalists were named.

The number of Semifinalists allocated in each state or selection unit is about one half of one percent of the graduating high school seniors in that state or unit. This selection procedure results in a group of Semifinalists representative of outstanding students throughout the entire nation.

A Semifinalist becomes eligible for Merit Scholarship consideration by attaining Finalist status. To become a Finalist, a Semifinalist must (1) be a U.S. citizen or in the process of obtaining citizenship, (2) be enrolled as a full-time secondary school student, (3) be endorsed by his secondary school principal, (4) substantiate his NMSQT scores by an equivalent performance on a second test, and (5) supply NMSC with information about his school record, academic or other accomplishments and honors, leadership ability, and the like.

Taken from National Merit Scholarship Corporation, <u>Annual Report</u>, 1970 (Evanston, Ill., 1971).

DISTRIBUTION OF STUDENT FINANCIAL AID
RECIPIENTS BY SEX IN FISCAL YEAR 1972

Aggregate U.S. Summaries	Educational Opportunity Grants Program[a]	College Work-study Program	Defense Student Loan Program[b]
Number of male recipients	156,981	238,203	361,590
Percentage of male recipients	49.0	48.0	56.0
Number of female recipients	163,388	258,054	284,106
Percentage of female recipients	51.0	52.0	44.0
Total recipients	320,369	496,257	645,696

[a]The former Educational Opportunity Grants Program was replaced by new student financial aid programs, including the Supplemental Educational Opportunity Grants Program, on July 1, 1973.

[b]The name of the program was changed to the National Direct Student Loan Program on July 1, 1972.

Source: Department of Health, Education, and Welfare, Office of Education. Data sent in response to request by the author on December 14, 1975.

WOMEN IN APPRENTICESHIP--WHY NOT?
(an excerpt)

The trainee, the employer, and the occupation all derive benefits from using the apprenticeship system. It seemed reasonable to
extend the benefits to those less organized areas of employment
dominated by women in which there are no widely recognized standards for formal on-the-job training or certification once a truly
skilled level of competency has been gained.

It was here that the project met a roadblock. Apprenticeship
agency officials argued that if there were no existing formal apprenticeship or certification of licensing to practice an occupation, it
was most unlikely to be skilled and could not meet up to the complexity required of a trade for it to be recognized as apprenticeable.
For confirmation, the project was referred to the Dictionary of Occupational Titles.

This two-volume reference work produced by the Department
of Labor defines some 22,000 occupations in over 230 industries and
is the basis on which many public and private agencies evaluate prerequisites, career ladder criteria, and place in the classification
and compensation hierarchies of large organizations. The updated
1965 third edition uses a six-digit code to classify the 36,000 job
titles by occupation and the skill and complexity level demanded by
the job. The last three digits of the code rate each job for complexity in relation to data, to people, and to things. Analysts select
ratings from three fixed hierarchies of worker functions arranged
in a descending order of complexity. Each scale used assigns a
zero to the most complicated functioning and an eight to indicate that
the job demands no significant functioning in that area.

An 878 rating for a particular job, for instance, indicates that
it involves no significant function with data (the first 8), "serving"
in relation to people (the 7), and no significant functioning with things
(the second 8). "Serving" is defined as "attending to the needs or re-
quests of people or animals or expressed or implicit wishes of
people. Immediate response involved." The implication is that a

Taken from Patricia Mapp, Women in Apprenticeship--Why
Not?, U.S. Department of Labor, Manpower Research Monograph
no. 33, 1974.

job so defined can be performed successfully by anyone with mini-
mal prerequisites and almost no training and that it involves little
responsibility. An 878 rating signifies the lowest level of complexity possible in any job.

An examination of entries in the DOT revealed a cluster of
traditionally women's jobs, derivatives of mothering and homemak-
ing, whose ratings, when juxtaposed with ratings of other jobs, were
obviously grossly undervalued for complexity:

Foster Mother, 878
"Rears children in own home
as members of family."

Rest Room Attendant, 878
"Serves patrons of lava-
tories in store . . ."

Child Care Attendant, 878
". . . House parent, special
school counselor, cares for
group of children housed in
. . . government institution."

Parking Lot Attendant, 878
". . . parks automobiles
for customers in parking
lot. . ."

Home Health Aide, 878
"Cares for elderly, convales-
cent or handicapped persons."

Public Bath Maid, 878
". . . not quite as skilled as
Pet Shop Attendant, 877."

Nursemaid, 878

Delivery Boy (newspaper car-
rier) 868
". . . or closer in complexity and skill level to a
Mud-Mixer-Helper, 887."

Nursery School Teacher, 878*
"Organizes and leads activities of prekindergarten children, maintains discipline
. . ."

Marine Mammal Handler, 328
"Signals or cues trained
marine mammals. . ."

Nurse, Mid-Wife, 378

Hotel Clerk, 368

Homemaker (cross reference
Maid-General), 878

Barber, 371

---

*In Wisconsin, a "3-year license will be granted [a nursery
school teacher] upon evidence of completion of a 4-year course in a
school accredited for providing a professional major in the teaching
of nursery school children."

Kindergartner, 878
"Entertains children in
nursery . . ."

Strip-Tease Artist, 848
". . . entertains audience
by . . ."

Nurse, Practical, 878
"Cares for patients and
children in private homes,
hospitals."

Offal Man, Poultry, 887
". . . shovels ice into chicken
offal container . . ."

Nurse, General Duty, 378
"Rotates among various
clinical services of institution such as obstetrics,
surgery, orthopedics, out-
patient and admitting, pedi-
atrics, psychology and tuber-
culosis. May assist with
operations and deliveries."

Cosmetology, 271
Cosmetologists Apprentice, 271
"Provides beauty services
for customers"

Nurse, Private Duty, 378
"Contracts independently to
give nursing care . . . ad-
ministers medications (and)
independent emergency
measures to counteract
adverse developments . . ."

Undertaker, 168
"Arranges and directs
funeral services . . ."

A parent or parent substitute, even a Nursery School Teacher
(878) does not rate with the Dog Trainer (228)--job analysts having
presumably observed that children are rarely or never spoken to
(level 6 in the people hierarchy), persuaded (5), diverted (4), super-
vised (3), instructed (2), negotiated with (1), or mentored (0).
Neither does a parent or nursery school teacher have need of data
(9 [sic] being no significant function). Any foreman--of toy assembly
or a rug cleaning crew, for instance--rates a 1 on data because he
coordinates. Crews of children (being "packages" rather than
people) don't need their activities to be coordinated, it seems, even
in groups of 18+.
Parents, parent substitutes, and homemakers in fact juggle a
combination of jobs along with the human interaction, namely:

Cooking	Short Order Cook	381
Sewing	Sewing Machine Operator	482
	Seamstress	884
Laundering	Laundry Operator	884

Ironing	Mangler	885
Cleaning	Cleaner, Furniture	887
Driving	Chauffeur	883

They also tend or operate a number of machines (mixers, heaters, furnaces, polishers, ovens, etc.). Yet their rating in the DOT's "things" hierarchy was at the level 8.

The project advanced a strong case for review and reclassification of the many traditionally women's jobs associated with child-raising and interpersonal or home economics skills that are most frequently learned informally in unpaid work, and for a reexamination of the job analysis methods, purported to be impartial, that could lead to such distorted results. The Manpower Administration funded a research project in Wisconsin during the years 1971 to 1973 to begin the monumental task of review and to make recommendations as to job analysis methods.

CONGRESSIONAL DEBATE ON THE ERLENBORN AMENDMENT
TO EXEMPT PRIVATE UNDERGRADUATE EDUCATION FROM
THE ANTIDISCRIMINATION PROVISIONS OF TITLE IX,
EDUCATION AMENDMENTS OF 1972

The Chairman: The Chair recognizes the gentlewoman from
Oregon (Mrs. Green) to close debate on this amendment.

Mrs. Green of Oregon: Mr. Chairman, it was just stated that
if a new institution wanted to start out as a one sex institution that
would be prohibited. I beg to differ with my colleague. That is not
the case.

It has been said that this is an unwarranted intrusion on the
part of the Government into the administration of higher education
institutions. We all know that the Government has intruded now for
many years in the administration of all the schools, elementary and
secondary, and higher education. It has intruded in terms of the
Civil Rights Act. We now say you cannot discriminate against a person because of his race. If the Erlenborn amendment is adopted,
however, we say go ahead and discriminate on the basis that that
person is a woman.

Mr. Chairman, I am not going to expound at length on the few
doctors we have in this country because quotas have been established,
and women have been denied admission to medical schools. I am not
going to go into the fact of the small number of women lawyers because there have been quotas, and women have not been admitted to
law schools. But may I say to you that unless a woman is admitted
at the undergraduate level she is not going to be able to go on to the
graduate level, and do the caliber of work that she would like to do.
So admission at the undergraduate level is very important if we are
going to have more women at the graduate level.

Mr. Chairman, to summarize briefly, title X, at least as I
see it, is simply an assertion of the basic American belief in human
equality, and the title merely asks that universities and colleges act
in good faith with their historic promise so that American women will
be judged on an equal footing, on the basis of merit, as individuals
without the restraints, alibis, or subterfuges of a quota system, obvious or implied.

Taken from U.S. Congress, House, Congressional Record,
92nd Cong., 1st sess., vol. 117, part 30, pp. 39260-91.

Mr. Chairman, I ask that the Erlenborn amendment be defeated.

The Chairman pro tempore: The question is on the amendment offered by the gentleman from Illinois (Mr. Erlenborn).

Teller Vote with Clerks

Mrs. Green of Oregon: Mr. Chairman, I demand tellers.

Tellers were ordered.

Mrs. Green of Oregon: Mr. Chairman, I demand tellers with clerks.

Tellers with clerks were ordered; and the Chairman appointed as tellers Mrs. Green of Oregon and Mr. Erlenborn, Mrs. Mink, and Mr. Ashbrook.

The Committee divided, and the tellers reported that there were— ayes 194, noes 189, [and] not voting 48. . . .

ACTUAL AND PROJECTED PERCENTAGE DISTRIBUTION OF
ENROLLMENT IN VOCATIONAL EDUCATION
PROGRAMS, BY SEX, FISCAL YEARS 1970-77

	1970	1971	1972	1977 (Projected)
Total	100.0	100.0	100.0	100.0
By Level				
All programs				
Male	45.0	44.3	44.6	43.0
Female	55.0	55.7	55.4	57.0
Secondary				
Male	37.4	--	--	36.0
Female	62.6	--	--	64.0
Postsecondary				
Male	60.7	--	--	60.0
Female	39.3	--	--	40.0
Adult				
Male	53.9	--	--	52.0
Female	46.1	--	--	48.0
By Program				
Agriculture				
Male	--	95.9	94.6	92.0
Female		4.1	5.4	8.0
Distribution				
Male	--	55.3	54.7	54.0
Female	--	44.7	45.3	46.0
Health				
Male	--	12.3	15.3	17.0
Female	--	87.7	84.7	83.0
Home economics				
Male	--	7.2	8.4	10.0
Female	--	92.8	91.6	90.0
Office				
Male	--	24.5	23.6	25.0
Female	--	75.5	76.4	75.0
Technical				
Male	--	92.3	90.2	91.0
Female	--	7.7	9.8	9.0
Trades and industry				
Male	--	89.1	88.3	87.0
Female	--	10.9	11.7	13.0

Source: U.S. Department of Health, Education, and Welfare, Enrollment in Vocational Education, Fiscal Year 1972 (Washington, D.C., 1973).

179

SUGGESTED ACTION BY WOMEN AND WOMEN'S
GROUPS TO ACHIEVE EQUALITY OF
EDUCATIONAL OPPORTUNITY

Federal level. 1. In each state, organized women's groups should
call on their federal representatives and senators to support
legislation designed to end discrimination against women in
education and training. This would include:

a. Legislation to deny federal contracts, scholarships, or
other funds to any institution of higher education that does not establish a working plan for achieving equal undergraduate admissions,
by sex, within the next five years, including equal access to scholarship and student employment opportunities.

b. Legislation of tax reforms to deny tax exemption for private institutions that do not have equal admissions policies, by sex;
and to deny tax savings to donors offering gifts to such institutions.

c. Legislation to require the Department of Health, Education,
and Welfare to collect and publish appropriate data on sex distribution of school student population, faculty and administration, by sex.
(Although this was one of the suggestions of the President's Commission on the Status of Women [1971], data now being published appears
less informative in this regard than that of past years. Such data
are essential to monitor the progress being made toward equal educational opportunities.)

d. Legislation to fund in-service workshops within state departments of Employment Security, and within federal manpower
agencies, to overcome sex stereotyping in admissions to training
programs.

2. In each state, such women's groups should also:

a. Institute suits to force the Department of Health, Education, and Welfare to withhold funds from all state departments of
education that do not affirmatively recruit and admit young women
to vocational programs funded by federal dollars, so as to achieve
equal admissions within five years.

b. Institute suits to require the attorney general and the Justice Department to pursue sex-discrimination cases vigorously, in
cases where union/management apprenticeship programs present a
pattern of exclusion of women, so as to achieve equal admissions
within five years.

c. Support women candidates for Congress, and for executive and judicial posts at the federal level.

d. Publicize the voting record of legislators on women's issues--the Equal Rights Amendment, credit availability--so that women may vote their interests in economic and political areas.

e. Support child care legislation. Use of child care facilities is a matter of choice for women with adequate financial resources, but for many working women it is a sheer necessity.

State level. In each state, organized women's groups should:

1. Call on state legislators to restructure the state Department of Education to ensure equal educational opportunity at all levels of publicly funded schools, and in all courses; equal opportunity and encouragement for mathematics and physics courses; equal opportunity for sports programs; equal opportunity for shop, vocational, and technical courses, programs, and schools; equal encouragement of career aspirations for both sexes by guidance counselors.

2. Support women for top-level executive, legislative, and judicial posts, particularly in the field of education.

3. Encourage state officials in apprentice-training programs to publicize opportunities for young women in skilled trades.

4. Request the appropriate state education official to inform all institutions of higher education that degree-granting privileges will be withdrawn from those institutions that do not end sex-discriminatory admissions and financial aid practices within five years.

5. Request the appropriate state education officials to amend the requirements for teacher certification to include courses in human relations stressing the identification of cultural, racial, or sex-stereotyping.

Local level. In each city, town, or school district, individual women should:

1. Enter electoral politics, as supporters of women and men candidates who support women's issues, and as candidates themselves. (Do not underestimate your own ability or that of the woman next door.)

2. Discuss with school committee, superintendent, and principals the implementation of Title IX; the purchase of nonsexist texts from kindergarten through grade twelve; the encouragement of enrollment by both sexes in those programs of study that interest them, regardless of traditional stereotyping.

3. Work to raise the sights of young women to educational institutions, study programs, and occupations appropriate to their talents. Urge them to apply, and reapply, to those institutions or fields they choose.

BIBLIOGRAPHY

BOOKS

American Council on Education. Weighted National Norms for All Freshmen--Fall 1969. Washington, D.C., 1970, 1974.

Anastasi, A. Differential Psychology, rev. ed. New York: Macmillan, 1956.

Astin, Alexander. Predicting Academic Performance in College: Selectivity Data for 2,300 American Colleges. New York: The Free Press, 1971.

Astin, Helen S. The Woman Doctorate in America: Origins, Career and Family. New York: Russell Sage Foundation, 1969.

Becker, Gary. "Economics of Discrimination." In Labor Economics and Labor Relations, edited by L. Reynolds and Moser Masters. Englewood Cliffs, N.J.: Prentice-Hall, 1974.

Bowen, Howard. Economics of Labor Force Participation. Princeton, N.J.: Princeton University Press, 1969.

Bowles, Samuel. Schooling and Inequality from Generation to Generation. Cambridge, Mass.: Center for Education Policy Research, Report No. 8, 1971.

Burtt, Everett J. Social Perspectives in the History of Economic Theory. New York: St. Martin's Press, 1972.

Carnegie Commission on Higher Education. A Classification of Institutions of Higher Education. Berkeley, Calif., 1973.

_____. Opportunities for Women in Higher Education. New York: McGraw-Hill, 1973.

Cass, James, and Max Birnbaum. Guide to American Colleges. New York: Harper and Row, 1972.

College Entrance Examination Board. College-Bound Seniors, 1973-74. Evanston, Ill.: CEEB, 1974.

_____. Summary Report, 1972-73. Evanston, Ill.: CEEB, 1974.

Council for Financial Aid to Education. Handbook of Aid to Higher
    Education. New York, 1972.

_____. Survey of Voluntary Support of Education, 1973-74. New
    York, 1975.

Cross, Patricia. Beyond the Open Door. San Francisco: Jossey-
    Bass, 1971.

Curti, M., and R. Nash. Philanthropy in the Shaping of American
    Higher Education. New Brunswick, N.J.: Rutgers University
    Press, 1965.

deRivera, Alice. "On De-Segregating Stuyvesant High." In Sister-
    hood Is Powerful, edited by Robin Morgan. New York: Vin-
    tage Books, 1970.

Doermann, Humphrey. Crosscurrents in College Admissions. New
    York: Teachers College Press, Columbia University, 1968.

Dunlop, John T. "The Task of Contemporary Wage Theory." In
    Theory of Wage Determination, edited by John T. Dunlop.
    New York: St. Martin's Press, 1957.

Education Commission of the States. Higher Education in the States,
    Vol. 5, No. 1. Denver, 1975.

Ekstrom, Ruth. Barriers to Women's Participation in Post-Secondary
    Education: A Review of the Literature. Princeton, N.J.: Edu-
    cational Testing Service, forthcoming.

Flanagan, J. and Associates. The American High School Student.
    Pittsburgh: University of Pittsburgh, Project Talent, 1964.

Hansen, L., and B. Weisbrod. "Distribution of Costs and Direct
    Benefits of Public Higher Education: The Case of California."
    In The Daily Economist, edited by S. H. Johnson and B. Weis-
    brod. Englewood Cliffs, N.J.: Prentice-Hall, 1973.

Harvard University and Radcliffe College. Report of the Committee to
    Consider Aspects of the Harvard-Radcliffe Relationship that Af-
    fect Administrative Arrangements, Admissions, Financial Aid,
    and Educational Policy. Cambridge, Mass., February 26, 1975.

Haven, E. W., and D. H. Horch. How College Students Finance
    Their Education. Evanston, Ill.: College Entrance Examina-
    tion Board, 1972.

Holmes, Oliver W. Quoted in American Labor and Manpower Policy,
    edited by Ronald Wykstra and Eleanor Stevens. New York:
    Odyssey Press, 1970.

Hughes, Everett. "Higher Education and the Professions." In Con-
    tent and Context, edited by C. Kaysen. New York: McGraw-
    Hill, 1973.

Lester, Richard A. Antibias Regulation of Universities: Faculty
    Problems and their Solutions. New York: McGraw-Hill, 1974.

National Academy of Sciences. Doctorate Recipients from U.S.
    Universities, 1956-66. Washington, D.C., 1967.

National Merit Scholarship Corporation. Annual Report, 1970.
    Evanston, Ill., 1971.

National Science Foundation. Federal Support to Universities, Col-
    leges, and Selected Nonprofit Institutions, FY 1973. Washing-
    ton, D.C., 1975.

Orlans, H. "The Effects of Federal Programs on Higher Education."
    In A Statistical Portrait of Higher Education, edited by S.
    Harris. New York: McGraw-Hill, 1972.

Perry, A. R., B. E. Anderson, R. L. Rowan, and H. R. Northrup.
    The Impact of Government Manpower Programs, in General,
    and on Minorities and Women. Philadelphia: Industrial Re-
    search Unit, Wharton School, University of Pennsylvania, 1975.

Reich, Michael. "The Economics of Racism." In Labor Economics
    and Labor Relations, edited by L. Reynolds and Moser Masters.
    Englewood Cliffs, N.J.: Prentice-Hall, 1974.

Rosenthal, Robert, and Lenore Jacobson. Pygmalion in the Class-
    room. New York: Holt, Rinehart and Winston, 1968.

Solmon, L. C., and P. J. Taubman, eds. Does College Matter?
    New York: Academic Press, 1973.

Thresher, Alden. College Admissions and the Public Interest. New
    York: College Entrance Examination Board, 1966.

Walsh, Patricia. "An Analysis of the Participation by Female Stu-
     dents in the Benefits of the Bundy Program." Unpublished
     study, Boston University, Department of Economics, June
     1975.

Willingham, Warren. Free Access Higher Education. New York:
     College Entrance Examination Board, 1970.

Women on Words and Images. Dick and Jane as Victims. Prince-
     ton, N.J.: Women on Words and Images, 1972.

Woodrow Wilson Foundation. Annual Report, 1970. Princeton,
     N.J., 1971.

                    JOURNALS AND PERIODICALS

Anderson, R. "What Makes a University Great?" Palo Alto, Calif.:
     Stanford University, 1974.

Bok, Derek. Harvard Today, Fall 1974, p. 10.

Freedberg, S. Harvard Crimson, March 27, 1973, p. 1.

Giroud, Francoise. Boston Globe, October 29, 1974, p. 20.

Goldberg, Philip. TransAction, April 1968, pp. 28-30.

Goodman, Ellen. Boston Globe, July 9, 1974, p. 27.

Hughes, John. "Who Should Pay for College Education?" Boston
     University Business Review, Winter 1958.

Richmond (Va.) News Leader, January 22, 1974, p. 14.

Shanahan, Eileen. New York Times, July 6, 1974, pp. 1, 7.

Stanford Observor, Stanford University, March 3, 1973.

Touhey, John C. "Effects of Additional Women Professionals on
     Ratings of Occupational Prestige and Desirability," Journal of
     Personality and Social Psychology 29, no. 1 (1974): 86-89.

Urdang, Stephanie. Boston University Daily Free Press, September
     27, 1974.

Van Horn, Edie. "At Large" by Mike Barnicle, Boston Globe, July 2, 1975.

Weidenbaum, Murray. Boston Globe, August 4, 1974, p. A-91.

GOVERNMENT PUBLICATIONS

Bryan, Gail. Discrimination on the Basis of Sex in Occupational Education in the Boston Public Schools. Boston: The Mayor's Commission on the Status of Women, 1972.

Coakley, Joanne. "Attitudes of Guidance Counsellors." In Report of the Massachusetts Governor's Commission on the Status of Women. Boston, 1972.

Commonwealth of Massachusetts. Report of the Massachusetts Governor's Commission on the Status of Women. Boston, 1972.

Equal Employment Opportunity Commission, Technical Information Division. "Total and Female Apprentices, By Trade or Craft, in Selected States, 1972." Tabulation, 1975, Washington, D.C.

General Accounting Office. "What Is the Role of Federal Assistance in Vocational Education?" Washington, D.C., December 31, 1974.

Public Laws. Washington, D.C.: U.S. Government Printing Office.

U.S. Congress. Congressional Record-House. November 4, 1971, pp. 39260-1.

_____. Hearings before the Special Subcommittee on Education of the Committee on Education and Labor. 91st Cong., 2d sess. on Sec. 805 of H.R. 16098. Parts 1 and 2., Discrimination Against Women. Statement of Dr. Bernice Sandler, Chair, W.E.A.L., pp. 300-10.

_____, House. Hearings before the Subcommittee on Equal Opportunities of the Committee on Education and Labor. H.R. 93rd Cong., 1st sess., on H.R. 208, Part I, p. 189 (July-September 1973); pp. 15-25; 187; 433-36; Lucy Sells, "A Pilot Test of Sex Differences in High School Mathematics Preparation." Appendix C, pp. 298-300.

U.S. Department of Commerce, Bureau of the Census. Characteristics of American Youth, 1974. C.P.R. Special Studies,
Series P23, No. 51.

_____. Characteristics of Population (1970), Table 57, Income in
1969, pp. 34-311.

_____. Educational Attainment, March 1972. Series P-20, No.
243, November 1972, Table E, p. 7.

_____. PC-1-634, 1970, Table 200.

U.S. Department of Health, Education, and Welfare, National Center
for Education Statistics. Earned Degrees Conferred, 1971-72.
Washington, D.C., 1972.

_____. Fall Enrollment in Higher Education, 1973. Washington,
D.C., 1975.

_____, Coleman, James. Equality of Educational Opportunity.
Washington, D.C., 1966.

_____, Wade, George H. Residence and Migration of College Stu-
dents: Basic State-to-State Matrix Tables, Fall 1968. Washington, D.C., 1970.

U.S. Department of Health, Education, and Welfare, Office of Education. Annual Report of the Commissioner of Education, 1971.
Washington, D.C., 1972

_____. Digest of Education Statistics, 1974. Washington, D.C.,
1975.

_____. Distribution of Student Financial Aid by Sex, 1972. Division
of Student Support and Special Programs. Washington, D.C.,
Tabulation, January 21, 1976.

_____. Financial Statistics of Institutions of Higher Education,
1969-70: Current Funds, Revenues, and Expenditures. Washington, D.C., 1972, pp. 5-6.

_____. "New Regulations to Protect Vocational Students." Boston
Globe, February 22, 1975; March 31-May 31, 1974.

_____. Residence and Migration of College Students, Fall 1968.
Washington, D.C., 1970.

_____. Statistics of Elementary and Secondary Day Schools, Fall
1973. Washington, D.C., March 1971.

_____. Summary Table, Aggregate U.S. Enrollment Fall 1974 and
Fall 1975. (Preliminary). Washington, D.C., December 1975.

_____. Trends in Post-secondary Education. Washington, D.C.,
1970.

_____. Vocational and Technical Education. Washington, D.C.,
annual report.

_____. Vocational Education Information I, II, III. Washington,
D.C., fiscal years 1972, 1973, 1974.

U.S. Department of Labor. "Decline of Sex Stereotyping in the
Skilled Trades." Monthly Labor Review. May 1974.

_____. Manpower Report of the President, 1963-75 (annually).
Washington, D.C.

_____. "Urban Family Budget Updated to Autumn 1974." Monthly
Labor Review. June 1975.

_____. Years for Decision, vol. II. Manpower Research Monograph
No. 24. 1974.

_____, Bureau of Apprenticeship Training. Women in Apprentice-
ship. Washington, D.C., August 1970.

_____, Mapp, Patricia. Women in Apprenticeship--Why Not? Man-
power Research Monograph No. 33. 1974.

_____, Sommers, Dixie. "Occupational Rankings for Men and
Women by Earnings." Monthly Labor Review. August 1974.

_____, Stevenson, Gloria. "Career Planning for High School Girls."
Occupational Outlook Quarterly. Summer 1973.

_____, Women's Bureau. Fact Sheet on the Earnings Gap. March
1975.

_____, Women's Bureau. Underutilization of Women Workers.
1971 Rev.

_____, Women's Bureau. Women's Handbook, 1969. Table 1.

_____, Women's Bureau. Women Workers Today. 1973 Rev.

ABOUT THE AUTHOR

BLANCHE FITZPATRICK is Associate Professor in the Economics Department of the Boston University College of Liberal Arts and teaches Labor Economics in the University Extension Program of Harvard University. She is a member of the Board of Trustees of Lowell University and a member of the Massachusetts Board of Higher Education, where she serves as Chairwoman of the Scholarship Committee. Her appointment in 1972 to the Massachusetts Governor's Commission on the Status of Women led Professor Fitzpatrick to further research on opportunities for women in training and education beyond high school and the effect of discriminatory admissions on lifetime careers and earnings.

Professor Fitzpatrick was previously employed as a Labor Economist in the Bureau of Labor Statistics of the U.S. Department of Labor and as an economic analyst in private industry. She has taught for over 15 years in Massachusetts and California.

Dr. Fitzpatrick received the A.B. degree from Tufts, the M.A. from Stanford, and the Ph.D. from Harvard, writing her dissertation on "Recurrent Unemployment in Manchester, New Hampshire." She has also published articles on the education of women and on the economics of aging.

EVALUATING VOCATIONAL EDUCATION--
POLICIES AND PLANS FOR THE 1970s:
With an Annotated Bibliography

Leonard A. Lecht

SEX AND CLASS IN LATIN AMERICA

edited by June Nash
and Helen Icken Safa

WOMEN IN ACADEMIA: Evolving Policies
Toward Equal Opportunities

edited by Elga Wasserman,
Arie Y. Lewin, and
Linda H. Bleiweis